IF THIS WERE FICTION

AMERICAN LIVES

Series editor: Tobias Wolff

IF THIS
WERE
FICTION

A LOVE
STORY IN
ESSAYS

JILL CHRISTMAN

University of Nebraska Press

Lincoln

Acknowledgments for the use of previously
published material appear on pages 211–12, which
constitute an extension of the copyright page.

The University of Nebraska Press is part of a land-
grant institution with campuses and programs on the
past, present, and future homelands of the Pawnee,
Ponca, Otoe-Missouria, Omaha, Dakota, Lakota, Kaw,
Cheyenne, and Arapaho Peoples, as well as those of the
relocated Ho-Chunk, Sac and Fox, and Iowa Peoples.

Library of Congress Cataloging-in-Publication Data
Names: Christman, Jill, 1969– author.
Title: If this were fiction: a love story
in essays / Jill Christman.
Description: Lincoln: University of Nebraska
Press, [2022] | Series: American lives |
Includes bibliographical references.
Identifiers: LCCN 2021053054
ISBN 9781496232359 (paperback)
ISBN 9781496233226 (epub)
ISBN 9781496233233 (pdf)
Subjects: LCSH: Christman, Jill, 1969– | Christman,
Jill, 1969– —Family. | Women college teachers—United
States—Biography. | Women authors, American—
Biography. | Artists—Family relationships—United
States. | United States—Biography. | BISAC: BIOGRAPHY
& AUTOBIOGRAPHY / Personal Memoirs |
BIOGRAPHY & AUTOBIOGRAPHY / Women
Classification: LCC CT275.C576 A3 2022 |
DDC 973.92092 [B]—dc23/eng/20220404
LC record available at https://lccn.loc.gov/2021053054

Set in Whitman by Laura Buis.
Designed by L. Auten.

The names of some individuals have
been changed to respect privacy.

For Mark

since feeling is first
who pays any attention
to the syntax of things
will never wholly kiss you;

wholly to be a fool
while Spring is in the world
my blood approves,
and kisses are a better fate
than wisdom
lady i swear by all flowers. Don't cry
—the best gesture of my brain is less than
your eyelids' flutter which says

we are for each other: then
laugh, leaning back in my arms
for life's not a paragraph

And death i think is no parenthesis

—E. E. CUMMINGS

Contents

IF THIS WERE FICTION

PART I

since feeling is first

THE SLOTH

There is a nothingness of temperature, a point on the body's mercury where our blood feels neither hot nor cold. I remember a morning swim on the black sand eastern coast of Costa Rica four months after my twenty-two-year-old fiancé was killed in a car accident. Walking into the sea, disembodied by grief, I felt no barriers between my skin, the air, and the water.

Later, standing under a trickle of water in the wooden outdoor shower, I heard a rustle, almost soundless, and looking up, expecting something small, I saw my first three-toed sloth. Mottled and filthy, he hung by his meat-hook claws not five feet above my head in the cecropia tree. He peered down at me, his flattened head turned backward on his neck.

Here is a fact: a sloth cannot regulate the temperature of his blood. He must live near the equator.

I thought I knew slow, but this guy, this guy was *slow*. The sound I heard was his wiry-haired blond elbow, brushed green with living algae, stirring a leaf as he reached for the next branch. Pressing my wet palms onto the rough wooden walls, I watched the sloth move in the shadows of the canopy. Still reaching. And then still reaching.

What else is this slow? Those famous creatures of slow—the snail, the tortoise—they move faster. Much. This slow seemed impossible, not real, like a trick of my sad head. Dripping and naked in the jungle, I thought, *That sloth is as slow as grief.* We were numb to the speed of the world. We were one temperature.

3

GOING BACK TO PLUM ISLAND

The decision to return to the island began with the dreams. Chad was back, and this time he hadn't come just for me. He was after my nine-year-old daughter, Ella.

Part of me had always known this would happen.

In my twenties and thirties I had tried to write Chad if not into complete obliteration then at least into insignificance. Here are the facts: As close as I can align the memories and the photographs with the markers of time—birthdays, moves, my mother's sequential boyfriends and waitressing jobs—Chad molested me, regularly and sometimes violently, from the time I was six or seven to age twelve, when the arrival of my period and the fear of pregnancy scared me so much I finally made him stop. I locked myself in the only room with a phone, and I hissed through the crack in the door that if he didn't stop, I would call my mother at the restaurant.

And he did. He stopped.

Was it that easy?

Chad was seven years older than me and twice my weight. He carried his wallet on a chain and a folded knife in the pocket of his saggy jeans. The feature I remember most about Chad's body is that he had no hips, no ass, nothing to hold up his pants, and so he wore a thick, brown belt with a buckle he'd forged himself (it had something menacing on it—a serpent? a skull and cross-bones?), cinched tight on the bones of his pelvis.

When I think of Chad physically, I see two things: His hands, which were never clean because of the work he did on engines. Even in deep memory, I feel the hands more than I see them, sandpapering the soft skin of the child's body I inhabit there, scratching audibly across the denim of my overalls. In close-up, there are the black whorls of his fingerprints as if he'd come, every time, from a booking at the station.

And I see him walking away. I think this is from all the times he'd cross the sandy field between his garage and our house, a straight view from my bedroom window. I would hide in my room while he knocked on the front door, hide without breathing, a rabbit in the grass, and then, when I thought it was safe, I would peek out from the lower edge of my window.

I wanted to watch him go.

I don't know how tall Chad was, but he loomed, a shambling Lurch from *The Addams Family*, shoulders hunched forward, pants hanging in a straight line from his belt down to his dirty sneakers, long legs moving in pendulum swings across the sand. He could cross a lot of ground with what appeared to be very little effort. Is there such a thing as an ambling lope? A stride both low-energy and efficient? Yes, I think so. This is the locomotion of a wolf, or a big cat—a predator.

Watching Chad walk away in memory, I see the animal in him, and from this perspective, and the supposed safety of over thirty years, I can almost find a fragment of empathy. He looks so broken and lonely, barely more than a kid himself.

And then I remember that the sag in his shoulders was disappointment. He hadn't found me. Now what would he do to get off? The empathy is gone and the rage is back.

Once, when I was in graduate school, a fiction-writing professor said to the class: "You should know everything about your characters. You should know what your characters look like walking away." And in that seminar room in Alabama, the lemony smell of azaleas drifting in through the cracked windows, so far away from that cold island in Massachusetts, the image of Chad walking back across that field hit me like a blow to the gut. *Yes*, I thought, *okay. I know.*

The dreams I could not shake had their roots in these days I escaped. In the dreams, he's outside, and I'm in, and he's trying to see if I'm in there. It's the most fundamental of nightmares: he's trying to get me. That's it. And no matter what I try to do, he can see me. I try to press myself up against the wall under the window, away from any possible line of vision, but my foot splays out to betray me, or he pushes right through the window and looks straight down to find my curled body, as small as I can make myself but not small enough. And then at some point in the dreams, I realize he's seen me, the jig is up, but he leaves me there. It's not me he's after.

Oh no. *No no no.* This time, Chad is back, and he's come for Ella.

Night after night, I burst from these dark dreams with the feeling that someone had cracked through my chest and was squeezing my heart. I couldn't get a breath, I felt like I was going to throw up, and I was so *mad*. I thought I was done with all this. I really did. "Oh, honey," my husband, Mark, would say in the morning when I told him, holding his arms open for me. "I'm so sorry."

But Mark didn't know what to do to help me, and at first, I didn't either. The dreams started in the summer and stayed with me through the fall and into winter. Crap. These intrusive fucking nightmares didn't fit into the recovery narrative I'd crafted for myself, and I was pissed. I thought I had written myself through all of this. Isn't that what I'd been telling people? Telling *myself*? That the writing had healed me? And hadn't I thought my recovery, once achieved, would last forever? Didn't I consider myself a kind of superhero of sexual abuse survival? Me with my wonderful family and happy sex life? The bulimia and binge drinking of my young adulthood now a mere vestige of a former self, I knew how to love and be loved. I'd moved from being a victim of my own sad brain, a captive in a body that remembered more than I did, to being a mother and wife, a friend and teacher, a woman with a big smile and a big heart who could stand steady and do the good work of helping others tell *their* stories. While I'd had my share of therapists in the beginning, I confidently attributed the mother lode of my emotional and psychological health to having written myself through childhood trauma in my first book.

In grad school, I had denied that the writing did me any good. My MFA program didn't have a nonfiction track, so I wrote my memoir under the cover of the short stories I brought in for workshop after a few of my peers accused me of perpetrating something they called "therapy writing." That made me furious—and nervous. I was afraid, of course, that maybe they were right. So I denied it. I denied that writing my childhood did me any good at all. Stamping my outraged feet and downing beer after beer at the bar after class, I insisted that my art was as legitimate as their art, that I was as distant from the Jill in my book (a typographical mark! the letter *I*!) as they were from the characters in their purportedly made-up stories.

But three years after the book was published, I visited a class of high school students. A girl with eyes I recognized from the mirror asked if writing my memoir had helped me, and I looked at her, and instead of releasing the tired lie that was waiting in my mouth like a dog by the door, I thought about her question. Had writing *Darkroom* helped me?

And I said for the first time: "Yes. Writing *Darkroom* saved my life." And when I heard myself say that, I knew it was true, so I kept talking. "In order to write that story the way I needed to write that story, I needed to look into all the dark corners of my brain. In order to find something true that would matter, I needed to think hard about things I'd avoided thinking about all my life. And now? Now the dark corners are lit up. Now I'm not carrying around this brain that holds things I'm afraid to look at." The girl smiled. "Try it," I said, and I hope she did.

What I wasn't ready to articulate then is my understanding that good writing and good therapy share similar goals and methods. In both, our objective must be to make some sense of a disorderly world. To do this, to find peace in the mess of it all, to make art out of anecdote, we have to *look closely*. We have to look past what we've grown comfortable with seeing, beyond the easy representations we allow to stand in for the real deal. We have to locate patterns and connections we didn't know were there. In this way, in both (good) therapy and writing, we work our way to a kind of cohesion, an order in the senselessness we can live with.

To survive, we might bury our traumas or skirt the edges of our grief, but to *heal*, we have to go right through the middle. We have to know what's in the dark places. We have to point to who scares us and see what makes us sad—give them all names. There's no other way through. I thought I had done this and emerged on the other side into the light. And yet, all through the winter, the dreams kept coming.

"Have you ever seen a match burn twice?" Chad asked, striking the wooden match on the rough bricks of the fireplace, both of us watching the flame between us, orange and blue.

"No."

He blew out the match and held the fading tip to my forearm. A blond hair sizzled and crimped.

"Oww! Hey!"

"Now you have."

I can never see his face. I know he had big glasses, and the outline of those frames stands in for the rest of his features, a kind of comic-book representation for both memory and dreams.

In the year Chad came back, Ella's favorite pajamas were a soft white cotton printed with hundreds of tiny pink ballet shoes, close fitting in the way that the manufacturers would have us believe will save our children in a fire. When I tiptoed into her room to make sure she was sleeping, Ella looked as if someone had come and stretched her in the night, pulling our little girl from chubby, bookish child into a lean, preteen body, muscled and limber from hours of dance class. She looked so impossibly beautiful, her dark eyelashes fringing her pale cheeks, her every limb a study in form, the tiny ballet shoes patterning her body in the crack of light from the door like the last pixies of childhood who did not want to leave. And that's when I started to think. *Nine. By the time I was nine . . .* And that's when Chad returned.

I imagined what I would do. I would kill to protect Ella. I would rip him limb from limb.

Some weeks, he would come every night, looking for Ella in the corners of my own damn brain. This could not be. This could not stand.

That's when I decided I needed to go back. I had to do something, and going back to Plum Island, where it all went down, was all I knew to do. The timing was perfect. In early March I would be attending a conference in Boston. I could slip away a day early, get a rental car, bring a friend who loved me enough to hear my problem and my proposal over the phone and climb onboard, and drive the hour north to Plum Island.

That was the extent of my plan. I should have thought it through. What exactly did I think I was going to *do*?

There is so much about this story that is hard to make clear. In the months after the door-crack-I'll-call-my-mother confrontation, Chad evaporated from our lives. Poof. Gone. Where he had once been a fixture, he was an empty space, nothingness.

Was it that easy? Would it have always been that easy?

My mother asked about him from time to time. "Where's Chad? Seems like we haven't seen him in a long time." And my brother, Ian, who was a couple years younger than Chad, shrugged his shoulders. "He's over there," he'd say, meaning in the double garage behind Chad's mother's house where Chad had set up a metal- and woodshop on one side—he'd been a student at the vocational technical high school—and a creepy living-room-drug-den-bedroom on the other side. The bed in the way back was built right into the wall, and there were wooden platforms to hold incense and candles. "He's over there," my brother said, and I, knowing more, said nothing at all, marveling at the possibility that my threat, a twelve-year-old girl's scared whisper against a nineteen-year-old boy's rough hands on the door, had made a difference.

For months, I startled at every sound, even silence. This was a new reality that could not hold, I worried. He must be planning something. He must be angry. Under the fear, then, was this spark of something else: if it was that easy, if all it took was a single threat, why hadn't I made Chad stop years ago?

The answer to this question was simple: I didn't know I could. I had no idea I had that kind of power. I was a child. How could I have understood what I now know about how pedophiles choose their victims? When my mother left me alone to go to work, I was vulnerable, an easy target. My threat to tell changed everything. So in addition to the precarious sense of relief I felt in Chad's absence, I felt two more things: shame (I could have stopped him and I didn't, so therefore I must have wanted it) and regret (I could have stopped him, I could have stopped him, I could have stopped him). Having Ella and watching her grow up across the years of childhood, the same years in my own memory shadowed by Chad, turned my perspective once again.

At nine, I had felt so . . . *grown up*. In my early twenties, when memories of Chad first surfaced—not exactly the *recovered memories* the media likes to debunk and call false but *insistent* memories, memories that would no longer permit me to look away or forward—I had felt as if perhaps I'd participated in something that was at least partially my choice, a very early consensual sexual relationship. These things that Chad did to me were mine to accept, mine to conceal, and thus my shame to hold. Since memory, always, is suspect, I was forever running over the years in my mind, wondering if "sexual abuse" was a mislabeling, but watching Ella, the first child I have ever truly seen grow up, I aligned birthdays with human socio-sexual development. At nine, my daughter's body was just starting to mature, but she was so clearly a *child*. Despite her preternatural interest in current events, civil rights, and the welfare of animals, Ella's birthday wish was for a meticulously themed Harry Potter party, complete with sealing-wax invitations, Quidditch, and—the highlight—a potions class.

"Veritaserum," I had explained from beneath the wide brim of my witch hat, "impels those who swallow it to tell the truth. If your potion turns green, you'll know your recipe has been a success. You can ask your friend anything you want, and your friend will *have* to tell you the truth."

The black-robed kids gathered around the ping-pong table on the second floor of the YMCA, and I watched as they poured their medicine cups of yellow vinegar and blue baking soda solutions together, the potions bubbling up over the rims, and they turned to one another with questions that needed answering. Ella's cheeks glowed a happy pink with the success of her party. Every child's brew frothed a gorgeous, oobleck green, and I thought, *Actually, veritaserum extracts the truth as the teller understands it. That's not the same thing.* Truth is complicated, and we all know that facts can lie. There is always a level *more* true: true, truer, truest—and then something beyond that we will never reach. How true is true enough?

Was I afraid of Chad? Yes. Truth. Was I more mad than afraid? Yes. Maybe. Was I going back to Plum Island to protect Ella or to save myself? Yes and yes. Was there a better way? I just didn't know.

All this to say: I don't know what makes Chad go away and what brings him back, but that spring he was back, and I needed to find a way to banish him for good.

The summer after I unleashed my desperate, furious power and Chad stopped coming around, my brother graduated from high school and my mother sold our house. I don't remember moving day, or even the weeks leading up to it—the sorting and the packing and the decision to leave our dog, Tigger, with the new owners of the house. She was an old dog, my mother argued, too old to give up the beach and move to the mountains. But move we did—leaving Tigger and Chad behind on the island—and I don't remember Chad coming over to say good-bye. I never saw him again.

When we were thousands of miles away, all the way across the country, I let myself relax a little, and then I did myself one better: I let myself forget. The repression of memory is never as simple as its pseudo-scientific detractors would have us all believe. Pulling out the psychological shovel and burying what hurts us isn't a quackish anomaly—it's human nature. Look around. Look inside. And the process of uncovering traumas from our past that we have managed to avoid really seeing for many years is not some kind of therapeutic voodoo. Far from it.

Our house on Plum Island was the very last one before the Parker River Wildlife Refuge. Our backyard was the entire refuge with its salt marshes and dunes and beaches. I can't imagine a more beautiful place to grow up, and yet, somehow in the seventies, our island was undiscovered, undeveloped. Like so many of the houses on the island at that time, the house my mother bought for $14,000 was no showplace—wide-plank floors, unfinished walls, visible studs and insulation—but my mom made it beautiful with staple-gunned fabrics over the ugly bits, a new coal-burning stove that formed the cozy center of the house, art made out of sea glass, driftwood, and shells.

To the kids at school, in the town across the bridge where we traveled on the bus, we were "the island kids," which translated to the poor kids, the grubby kids, the good-for-nothing kids. Our island was a kind of a ghetto, the wrong side of the river, but man, what a *location*. We picked wild cranberries from the bogs and gathered buckets and buckets of bayberries to melt down into a single candle. We fished in the marshes and made elaborate forts in the dunes. We swam, we climbed, we ran free.

Friday nights began with a bicycle ride to the island store with a dollar to stock up. A penny a fish. That's one hundred Swedish Fish in yellow, red, and green, sometimes stopping short of the full paper bag of fish for an Atomic Fireball or a comic-wrapped powdery pink block of Bazooka bubblegum, for tongue-on-fire excitement and longevity, respectively. The only TV in the house was balanced on a wooden fishing crate in my room—an old ten-inch RCA sporting rabbit-ear antennae, tips flagged with aluminum foil.

Friday night was the best night on TV—first *The Love Boat* and then *Fantasy Island*. Sometimes my brother was with me, but mostly I watched alone. How I longed to be Julie with her clipboard, beaming at the top of the gangway as she welcomed that week's guests to the *Pacific Princess*, keeping everything straight and in order—her uniform and hair, each passenger's name and quirky predilections, an elaborate schedule of fun and enriching activities and destinations. And as if *The Love Boat* weren't escape enough, next, a show with a wish-fulfillment premise, a show with *fantasy* right in the title, a show in which hearts could be unbroken, fortunes recovered, and childhoods replayed. There was much time travel. Complete do-over. Did I cringe when Tattoo climbed up on his tower to throw his insubstantial weight onto the bell rope and shout out in his much-parodied French accent, "De plane! De plane!"? No. No, I did not. I laid out what was left of my Swedish Fish, rationed for the second part of my Friday night double feature, and felt a shiver of pure pleasure.

It sounds lonely, but it really wasn't. Being the kid who was me on Plum Island in the seventies had dangers, but it wasn't all bad, and that's important. On Friday nights, while my mom was off serving chili and beer to keep our small family afloat, I fell into the fantasy on the screen with uncomplicated joy, and now I wonder if I'd always known I would get away from Chad. Maybe even more than once.

In Boston, the day before we were supposed to get the car and drive north to the island, the winds were whipping and the snow was coming down. If the voicemail messages from both Mark and my mother I listened to after my last meeting of the day were any indication, conditions on the island were much worse. Mark was fairly calm: "It sounds like there's another storm coming through. You might want to take another look at the forecast." My mother, who had never before called me on my cell phone when I was working, sounded panicky: "You can't go to Plum Island! There's a TERRIBLE storm! They've called in the National Guard. On TV they're showing a house that fell into the ocean. FELL INTO THE OCEAN!"

Really? I thought. *Really?* And then: *Now you worry, Mom? Now?*

My friend Sherrie had signed on months earlier when I told her about the dreams. Sherrie is a poet and a genius with fabric and beads, a dear friend whom I met at my first post-MFA job and who has managed to appear like a kind of steady angel in my greatest moments of need since then. Also, Sherrie didn't think I was nuts to need to physically return to confront the past. Adopted as a baby with her twin sister when she was an infant in 1969, Sherrie had recently made the decision to search for her birth mother, despite her twin's objections. Her sister wanted to live only looking forward, but Sherrie needed to look in all directions—including back. We understand each other.

In our hotel room, I checked the weather—looked clear for the next day—and then I pulled up the news. Yup. Sure enough. Sherrie and I sat shoulder to shoulder on the bed and watched footage of a house along an eroded stretch of beach, pounded by the waves, slowly slowly slowly tipping over the edge. Geez. Was this an omen that we should stay away?

Ninety percent of me was relieved. Here was the perfect excuse. The weather was formidable, the island was impassable. I had *wanted* to go back, but now I couldn't. Too bad. Maybe the bridge would be closed. What kind of metaphor was that?

Shit. The remaining 10 percent was scared. Did this mean Chad had won? Did this mean the dreams would never stop? Was it possible that chickening out would somehow leave Ella vulnerable? Does the world work like that?

The weather wasn't the only thing I checked online before the trip. Months earlier, when the dreams intensified, I had done what I could to find Chad, hoping—forgive me, but it's true—hoping I would learn that he was dead, something which, if his teenaged lifestyle choices (drugs, alcohol, fighting, motorcycles) had continued unchecked, seemed fully possible. I'm no kind of private detective, but I was able to determine from some online record searching that his mother had been dead for over a decade, and it looked as if his most current address was in Salisbury, at least twenty minutes away, but I couldn't find a record of sale on their Plum Island house. I didn't really know *where* he was, but I was pretty sure he was still alive. Going in, I knew my chances were good that I would not find him on the island, and if I didn't, I had no intention of trying to track him down in Salisbury.

How do I explain this? I wasn't looking for Chad himself, fifty years old and in God knows what condition after what I assumed was some pretty serious substance abuse and hard living. I was looking for the memory of Chad—and then, somehow, I was going to find a way to slip free of its dark snare.

The next morning, when I pulled back our curtains on the twenty-seventh floor, the world was *sparkling*. No excuses. We would go.

Newburyport is the last town before you cross the river for the island, and Sherrie and I started there. I needed to ease myself into the past, and breakfast in Newburyport seemed right. At first, I felt comfortably like a tourist in my own childhood, and this phrase looped through my head as we wrapped our scarves tighter around our necks to walk along the dock, edged by a park

I'd never seen, and then navigate the slushy streets to Angie's Food: *I am a tourist in my own childhood.* I couldn't stop to think what my brain might have meant by this. A tourist is a visitor. A tourist gets to leave.

The last time I saw Newburyport, I was thirteen, so there was the thrill of rediscovery after so many years: the now-defunct Fishtail Diner where Fast Eddie had cracked our eggs, four at a time, before we struck out for the open seas on my mother's boyfriend's fishing boat; the toy store—the *same* toy store!—where I'd picked out wind-up toys and kites; the newsstand where my mother's friends had spent long hours drinking coffee refills and eating tuna melts; the dock with its giant scale for giant fish. So there was the excitement of recognition. And the horror of the same.

At Angie's, I ate the eggs Benedict recommended by the super-friendly Enterprise employee who'd helped us get our bags into the trunk of our economy Ford. When he'd asked where we were headed, and I'd said, "Newburyport. I grew up on Plum Island, and I haven't been back in thirty years," he smiled and nodded his head like he'd just passed me a joint and he was holding the smoke in his lungs, letting the high soak in. "*I'm* from Newburyport!" he said with a burst of breath and a grin, and because this whole day, this whole journey, had a scrim of the other-worldly and predestined from the get-go, I thought, *Of course you are.* He told us what he loved about the island where I'd run wild as a kid, how when he was a teenager they'd drive out there at night and build fires low in the dips between the huge and shifting dunes. "Down where nobody could see us. It was awesome. And then we'd do things we probably shouldn't have been doing." He grinned again.

I told him I wanted to have lunch at a place called The Grog, where my mother used to be a waitress, and how I'd ride my banana-seated yellow bike over the bridge and into town by myself every Sunday to visit her there, eating cups of chili heaped with shredded orange cheese and sipping an endless procession of Shirley Temples slid across the polished wooden bar by Bruce the

Bartender. "The Grog's still there," our new friend said, handing over his card and telling us about the Mexican restaurant on the main street. "But if you want a buzzy afternoon, just drop my name here and they'll hook you up with some free margaritas."

I was old enough to think, *Wait. Aren't you renting us a car?!* And I was *me* enough to appreciate his enthusiasm for our pilgrimage. "A lot of things have changed," he said, closing the trunk and shaking our hands. "You'll see. A lot of things."

As soon as we crossed over the drawbridge, I felt a kind of tingling in my bloodstream. Every molecule: fight or flight. Dark corners of the brain I hadn't known were still there. Language loosening, scenes intruding. Here. Under the bridge. Giving me a ride home, Chad had swung his car down this road, into the marsh under the bridge, a troll with his reeking, smoky breath. Scenes and images flashed. The nightmare felt real. Now *I* was back. But who was I? Why had I come?

I moved my lips to the words without sound: *I am a tourist in my own childhood.* Instead of turning right off the bridge, the road that would take us to my end of the island, I asked Sherrie to go straight. Just a block. I wanted to see if the island store was still there. The candy. I wanted to buy some Swedish Fish. This was an obvious stall technique, but Sherrie obliged, looking at me warily. "I'm okay," I assured her. "I feel okay. If I'm not okay, I'll tell you."

Inside Dick's Variety (Grocery Deli Tobacco Ice Cream Subs News), the glass case under the cash register was still filled with candy: Jujubes, Boston Baked Beans, Now and Later, Airheads, Nerds, Jolly Ranchers—and Swedish Fish. Just the red ones, pre-packaged in yellow. Pulling out two dollars for what couldn't have been more than twenty fish, I joked with the cashier wearing the blue-and-orange knit cap: "In my day, the candy here was a penny." As she took the bills from my hand, she laughed a laugh deepened by years of smoking, the fact that I was back after thirty years away not even really worth noticing, and flipped a thumb to the side: "Yeah. Things sure have changed, but we still have our pickle barrel!" An old-timer hanging out at the end of the counter joined in with a smoky baritone chuckle—*we still have our pickle barrel!*—and I peered down at the pickles jostling one another like fetal pigs in a formaldehyde bath, waiting for the ladle, the dissection. I swallowed back a gag, my tongue sour with memory before we'd even left the candy store.

I was no longer a tourist. I was ten, and I was going home.

On Google Maps, I'd confirmed that our old house on that prime real estate had been torn down, replaced by a three-story beauty, a million-dollar home where our glorified shack had once stood. We'd start with Chad's. Just as I knew my house was gone, I knew his was still there. Returning to one's childhood in the age of satellite and internet means virtual reconnaissance is possible. I was armed with information—partial, uncertain, but still something—and yet I had no plan. The extent of my plan was to trust my gut and to show Chad I was not afraid. I was all grown up, and damn it, I was fierce. I was not to be fucked with by the likes of him.

"Okay," I said. "Okay." I directed Sherrie the half mile or so to Chad's street, the street before mine, which was the last street before the refuge. Navigating the narrow road between the snow banks—when had the roads shrunk?—Sherrie's toe barely tapped the gas pedal as we crept along. I felt furtive. It was as if I were turning the pages of my childhood, driving along sketched-in, charcoal roads in a real car. You weren't supposed to be able to do something like this. My mother's best friend's old house wasn't the same. Somehow, it looked bigger. Had it always been two stories? I only remembered one and an attic sort of space. Maybe the house had been renovated, pushed upward. The weathered gray New England shingles looked the same, the red trim.

Sherrie inched forward, watching me. Chad's house was next. "Okay," I said again. "I'm okay," I lied. First I saw the front of

Chad's house, and it was as if it were the only structure on the whole island that hadn't changed at all. In a landscape of brown tones and shingles, the pale-yellow siding of Chad's house was one of those things that was not like the others. White trim, black shutters, a door on the front I knew nobody used. Almost thirty-five years later, the fact that I knew the rules of this house was confirmed. In the deep snow of the postage-stamp front yard, there were no footsteps. No tracks to that unused front door.

I took a picture right then, and the photo is dirty snow, brown sand, gray roof, yellow house—all muted, tired—and then a flash of deep red in the side mirror that I recognize to be my wool coat. This fragment of me looks like a cardinal in a shrub. There was one shrub, for real, in front of Chad's house and an assortment of shrubby-looking beach pines around the edges of the property. I remembered these, but now they seemed bigger. Of course those that survived would have grown. We have all grown.

In my mind, I could see the inside of the house. All the shades would be drawn. The real way to go in or out was through the side door attached to the small porch. The first room was the living room with thick, stinky carpets, everything steeped in dense, stale smoke. The kitchen was really more of a kitchenette with a cheap ridge of laminate counter separating its small appliances from the room where the TV was always on. Then a tiny bathroom, Chad's room, and his mother's room.

Theirs was more of a beach cottage than a place two people would live, but without the quaintness, like a beach cottage out of some kind of apocalyptic hellscape. As children, we didn't go in there often, and only when Chad's mother—who worked long shifts at a mental hospital for the violently insane and told really creepy stories—wasn't there. I remember only one visit to Chad's room. He had said he wanted to show me something that was in the closet. I can see his hand on the door of the closet, the kind that slides to the side. White. That's all I remember. I don't remember what he showed me. I try, but there is nothing there.

Chad didn't sleep in that room, in the time I knew him anyway. He stayed in the garage. He did all his work in the garage.

That was Chad's lair, and as we crawled down Jackson Way, grisly images from inside the garage flashed in my brain: melting candles, burning incense, a giant vice with a throwing star clamped in its square metal jaws, sparks flashing from the file in Chad's big hand, heavy smoke over musky animal reek. I could smell him. My refrain was different now, and one I had trouble believing: *I am a grown-up. I am safe. I am a grown-up.* I was forty-three years old and locked in a rental car, for chrissakes. That's the kind of grown-up I was. I was the kind of grown-up who would attend a conference of many thousands of professionals, the kind of grown-up who would sit on the board of the association hosting that conference and then rent a car to drive up the coast before flying out the next morning to reunite with her grown-up professor husband and her two well-protected, beautiful children. I tried hard not to notice the thought that the kind of grown-up I was pretending to be, the kind of grown-up who would be safe in her rental car, would likely not be assessing her status as a grown-up. But never mind. I nodded wordlessly to Sherrie, and she maintained our steady progress. The car crept forward. "I'm okay," I said again. "I'll tell you if I'm not."

And now I could see around the corner. Everything was occluded. My view of the double garage was blocked by a jumbled assortment of vehicles and watercraft—a salt-eaten station wagon faced us, hooked up to a trailer bearing a sailboat, and next to that a huge white RV and another trailer, this one with two boats, skiffs, stacked gunwale to gunwale like a giant clam. *Okay, okay,* I thought. *Breathe.* I didn't recognize the car or the boats, and ridiculously, I took this as a comfort, although of course, that was absurd. A man can buy a new boat in the course of thirty years, can't he? But then I got a clear glimpse of the garage through the tunnel of cold air between the sailboat and the RV, enough to see a window I knew, with an air-conditioning unit duct-taped into the bottom half. I was in my nightmare. I couldn't get a breath. I would have opened the door to vomit, but I was afraid to touch the door. I was afraid to move my hand.

"Go," I whispered to Sherrie, digging deep for air. "Go. Go go go go go."

When you return to a childhood whose story was told on the shifting sands of a barrier island—and your house has been torn down and replaced with a different house, another kind of life entirely—it's hard to find your bearings. Sherrie and I circled the block and pulled into the dead end that was my street: Temple Boulevard. "I don't remember the trees being this big," I said to Sherrie when we got out of the car. I was crying.

She reached over and squeezed my arm. "What do you want to do?"

"Walk around," I said. "I just want to walk around a little." *Fuck, I was thinking. Fuck fuck fuck. Chad wins. I ran. I got close and I ran away. I am still afraid.* I had been dismantled by one glimpse of an old garage. *Fuck.*

There was nobody home in the big new house that stood regally where our one-story cottage had once squatted, and I guessed it was a beach getaway, not the kind of place, say, where people would weather a storm that was pulling houses into the ocean. I remembered the Storm of '76. The great nor'easter. How the National Guardsmen had come to our door, knocked, told us it was time to evacuate, but my mother said no, we couldn't. She had cookies in the oven, she explained to the baffled uniforms, and she needed to fold the fortunes inside as soon as they came out of the oven, while the cookies were still pliable. Thank you, but we'd stay. The morning after the worst of the storm, the beach had been covered with extraterrestrial-looking icebergs—honeycombed chunks of ice as big as park benches—and we walked among them, snapping pictures. Back in our cozy house, we drank cocoa and broke open our fortunes. My mother had written them herself, so they were all lucky.

I climbed the dune behind what had been our house but couldn't be sure if there was anything I really remembered. All the contours were different, the place where I'd sunbathed no longer there. At the top, I turned, and again I was struck a physical blow: a clear shot of the back of Chad's garage, the same angle as the view from my bedroom window when he walked away—the same shingles, the same lilting picket-and-wire fence, bent by the wind into a crooked spine, the same gray plywood nailed over the window in the exact corner where I knew the bed had been. It was as if this view had been preserved for me, not a blade of beach grass out of place. The boarded-up window was the thing I could not stand, so sinister. My heart. I was sick in my heart.

I raised my hand and pointed. Sherrie's eyes followed my finger.

"That's it," I said. "That's the garage. It looks exactly the same. That's it."

"Oh, Jillian," she said, moving closer to me. I rested in the circle of her protection. I knew if there was an attack—which is what every part of my body was expecting—she would be my fierce defender, and then I thought: *What if Chad is hiding from me? Could he be in there?* What if he was crawling along the dirty baseboards, scared that some part of his giant body might betray his location? *What if he is afraid of me?*

I needed to think. I needed a plan. I mean, how is a body supposed to know how to react in these completely bizarre scenarios? You've returned to the landscape of your childhood abuse. What are you supposed to *do*? I didn't know, but I knew I had to do *something*. I couldn't leave without doing something.

We drove through the gates and onto the refuge—and my mind let me play tourist again. I'd never had to *pay* before. All the beaches were closed because of the storm so we drove a few miles down to a marsh walk, parking among the birders with their poised binoculars. *We are all looking for something*, I thought. For the tenth time that day, Sherrie and I wished for more serious boots, but we tromped through the snow on the boardwalk to reach the marshes, climbing the clanging metal steps of a lookout tower and standing high in the brisk wind and bright sun— looking out. The blue of the river was deepened by the floating icebergs, so white in dark water, and where the river broke into tributaries, some so narrow a child could leap across them and make the other bank if she got a running start, the marsh grasses curved down the muddy banks like a velvet drape. I felt giant, huge, as if I could reach out a finger and smooth the edge of the grass tapestry down below.

"I need to go back," I told Sherrie. "I can't let him win. If I just run away, he wins. He still has me." High in the lookout tower, I got a grip, and I laid out my first real plan.

Back in the parking lot, I called Mark and told him what had happened, let him know we were about to go back. "You are *not* going into that garage," Mark said, his voice rising in my ear from one thousand miles away.

"He's not there," I said. "I'm sure he's not there." Pretty sure. Not totally sure.

"There could be someone even more dangerous living there now," Mark said. "I want you to promise that you won't go into the garage." Poor Mark. He sounded panicky. He wanted me to tell him the name of the street again.

"Jackson Way," I said. "And, okay. I don't think I need to go into the garage anyway. That would just be like torture. I don't need to see that much. All I'm going to do is knock on the door and tell whoever answers the door that I used to know someone who lived there when I was a kid and I want to look around a little. Just outside. I won't go in anywhere."

"Call me as soon as you do it," Mark said. "I love you."

"Okay. I love you."

I needed to let that place and its shadowing ghost—the grown man or the memory of the teenager who had hurt me—know I was not afraid. We parked in a gravel lot two houses down from Chad's and went over the plan. We'd walk back to the house together, Sherrie would wait in the street right behind me, but I would walk up to the house alone. And then I would knock. That was my whole strategy: I would knock.

The driveway had been cleared of snow all the way back to the boats, and the asphalt shone in the wet patches. From this close, I could see the dirt and mold that had collected in the ridges of the yellow siding. Everything except the shoveled ground, washed by the heavy snows, looked filthy. In my body was a war. Flight or fight, fear or courage, child or adult, 1979 or 2013. My body was the place two currents meet the ocean and rise up in a frothing ridge. I was the confluence. The storm door on the yellow house was a gate to hell. Sherrie's face at my side was the steadiest kind of love. I squeezed her hand and stepped forward. *Fuck it. I am not afraid. You don't scare me anymore, you asshole.*

Under this rage, I felt a giant upswell of love. I don't know what else to say. So much love. Sherrie, standing sentry right behind me; Mark back in Indiana with his hand on the phone; our kids safe in the room next to their father, building sturdy Lego towers with their interlocking blocks; my friends at home, waiting to hear how I fared; my friend Nikki, whom I'd seen at the conference, a sister survivor. I knew whatever I did in this moment, I would tell her, and I wanted my act to be the kind that would pull Nikki up with me. If I were in a movie, you would have watched as my walk toward that door gained force and speed. You would have seen my hand raise, the fist already formed, and you would have heard what happened next, the solid sound reverberating in the dark theater, me in my red coat lit up by the white snow, standing at the door of the dirty house: knock, knock, knock.

The response was immediate.

Two giant dogs peeled out of the dark entry to the rest of the house, barking viciously. I jumped and took a step back, my heart startling in its cage of ribs, watching the black frame behind the dogs for whoever might come next and hoping the rattling door would hold. The dogs threw themselves against the window, showing their teeth, spraying saliva on the pane.

I looked beyond the dogs and into the dark space from which they'd emerged. Nothing happened. No one came.

I hadn't thought this moment through. Hearing the dogs throw themselves at the door—muscle on metal, concussive, so loud—I concentrated on my own body, noticing my feet in the too-thin boots on the cold concrete, realizing I had planned only what I would say if a stranger opened the door: *Hello. I'm sorry to bother you, but I had a friend who used to live here. I wonder if you would mind if I just walked around the yard?* I didn't know what I would do if Chad himself emerged from the shadows, and yet, checking my body from my icy toes to my pounding heart, I thought, *I am not afraid. I am not afraid of you anymore.* And I knew how I could make this courage true.

Here we were again, each on our own side of a closed door, just as we had been over thirty years ago when I had told him to go away. And he had. Now that Chad was back, sulking into my night dreams, I had gone out in the bright winter sun to track him down where he lived—or where he used to live—and this time I would not cower. This time, I would protect Ella and save myself.

The dogs barked and growled. I stepped forward. I knocked again, louder this time. Behind me was all this love, this rising surge of love, and that love held me up and pushed me forward. The dogs lost their minds.

I had knocked—twice. No one came.

And that was that.

Whether I had found Chad himself or my memory of Chad, this time, I would walk away. This time, I would leave and not come back.

As I turned to walk the ten steps back to Sherrie, I felt a smile come to my face. A smile? "Nobody's home," I said, shrugging, as if that were the most inconsequential thing in the world. And then, "Actually, I'm thinking that's the best thing I could have hoped for, you know?"

My blood was tingling again, but this time, it felt loose, freed, the dam opened and the water pushing past into the open sea where it belonged. I didn't cry until I heard Mark's voice on the other end of the phone. "I did it," I said, and I told him about how I'd felt the love, a protective buffer of love.

"Oh honey," Mark said. "You're so brave. You're my hero."

On the day I returned to Plum Island, the National Guard was back again, too. Having finished what we'd come to the island to do, Sherrie and I decided to drive by and see the house that had fallen into the sea. I didn't have a good reason for wanting to look except that I'd never seen a house sideways in the waves, and the metaphorical possibilities seemed rich. The Guard had closed off a single stretch of road along the beach, right by my old bus stop where the cranky old lady in the housecoat used to live with her tiny gray dog. Gawkers had been coming to the island to get a close-up look at the destruction, and the guardsmen stood by their roadblock to turn outsiders away. This was somebody else's disaster to claim. When a guardsman leaned toward my open window and asked if we were residents, it would have been easy to lie—I wanted to see the house in the ocean—but instead I told the truth: "I used to live here," I said. "But not anymore. I don't live here anymore."

The guardsman in his fatigues didn't care about the details, didn't care that I'd returned to face disaster—or to change my vision of catastrophe, stare it down, grapple with my own domestic emergency. He shook his head, said nothing, took a couple of steps back, and made the universal gesture for "turn it around and get the fuck out."

Sherrie and I didn't care. I had knocked—twice. To celebrate, we went to The Grog and sat under the portrait of Duncan, a crazy old man I remember from my Shirley Temple–drinking days with Bruce the Bartender. Nostalgia be damned, I ordered a pint of IPA instead of an icy glass of grenadine syrup, but I still got the chili with cheese. It was as good as I'd remembered it, but one thing had changed: now they melt the cheese on top. In my day, it was a tumbling pile of shredded cheese that spilled over onto the glossy tabletop. You had to manage and stir it in as best as you could. I liked the cheese better the old way.

And the dreams? Back in Indiana with my family, I had a new dream. I dreamed I could fly. In forty-three years of dreaming, I had never flown. Not like this.

The place was beautiful, a kind of dream-flyer training camp staffed with carrier pigeons holding long colored ribbons in their beaks to show the dreamers in what order we would take off and land. At first, I was flying just below Mark's sister, Sophia, the athlete, and we were so far above the trees that wisps of clouds licked our cheeks, but they didn't feel cold or wet. Sophia said, "Look, I use my left hand like this—to steer," and that's when I noticed she was a lefty flier and I was a righty; when I reversed my own method, the one that was working just fine, to try it her way, I lost control and the fear of crashing was back.

So I went back to my method, and again I was alone, swooping, swooping. I felt completely free and unburdened in a way I never had—*not even in dreams*. I practiced a few backward somersaults, a flipping, weightless joy, arching my back and letting the wind lift me higher. I wanted to stay here, safe and buoyant, forever or a very long time, but it wasn't as if this place were entirely without rules.

The pigeons flew by, holding their different colored ribbons in their beaks. The pigeons were the dreamy, avian equivalent of the people in the reflector vests with the wands down on the tarmac, coming to lead me home, and since I was pretty aware of how fantastic this all was, I almost expected a Red Baron wink from the one in the front holding the long crimson ribbon in her beak. I watched the pigeons circle and dive—red, orange, yellow, all the colors of the rainbow—and after violet, I turned my hips a bit, finding the wave of air I'd need to follow my pigeon friends, as if I'd been doing this all my life. When we dropped below the clouds and into the river valley where we'd begun, I saw people on the river beach under the shining sun, cooling their toes in the water, and I thought, *Now I'll crack. Now the undoing, the loss of control, the fear of failure, crashing . . .* But the wind held me up—it was so easy. No flailing and no effort, everything airy and soft. When I splashed down with the merest ripple in the water in front of the friendly people on the beach, they clapped and cheered and congratulated me on my wonderful flight. There was a baby propped up in a pile of towels. Her open, toothless smile was a kind of signal to wake up, and I thought, *Wow. Wowwowwow. Hey there, baby, I flew!*

I keep three decapitated tassels of Plum Island beach grass in a miniscule square glass bottle balanced on the windowsill above the kitchen table where my children sit every morning to eat breakfast. Sometimes, when I'm spreading butter on Henry's bagel or handing Ella a spoon for her grapefruit, a glint in the morning sun catches my eye, and I follow the light up to the three disintegrating brown tufts. I'm pretty sure it's illegal to collect any artifacts—animal, vegetable, or mineral—from a national wildlife refuge, so in order to stuff the grasses covertly into my purse, I'd snapped off their frondy tips. While I was breaking the law, I'd scooped up an Altoids tin of sand and slipped that into my purse, too, making away with these relics of my feral childhood on this particular stretch of the Atlantic Ocean.

Why do I keep the grass and sand? Why did I bring them home? I think I mean for them to be talismans of a time when I not only rescued myself but lived in a kind of natural freedom I don't think I've known since—not even in my reckless teenage years on the mountain. It wasn't all bad. There was much to love on the island, so much to see, so much to learn. Plum Island was a lucky place to be a kid. One bad guy cannot destroy it all unless I let him, and when I look at the beach grass in my window, I remember how many ways there are to be saved.

A few months after my trip to Plum Island, the kids and I shared the Swedish Fish in a way that was completely unceremonious, and in that way, exactly right. Mark was off somewhere—teaching, I think—and we were sitting around the table after dinner. "What's for the dessert?" Henry wanted to know, and I looked in the pantry for something sweet, but nothing popped out at me. Nothing looked good. "Oh! I know," I said, and I went back to my bedroom, dug to the bottom of my underwear drawer, and extracted the hidden candy and the Altoids sandbox.

"Swedish Fish!" I said, returning to the table and ripping open the package. The kids beamed. As I dealt them out into three piles like cards—to be absolutely fair—I told them about my trip. How Mommy had gone back to Plum Island where *she* was a kid, and Aunt Sherrie had gone along to keep her company, and how the first thing we'd done when we got to the island was go to the store at the center of the island. When Mommy was little, there were things called penny candy counters with all different kinds of candy in baskets, and *everything* was a penny. One penny.

What kind of candy could you get for a penny, Ella wanted to know, and I counted off on my fingers. "Well, Swedish Fish, of course—in three different colors. Bazooka gum, Atomic Fireballs, Bit-O-Honey, Bottle Caps, Gobstoppers, Laffy Taffy, Smarties, Peppermint Patties, Zotz . . ." The kids wanted to hear more about this magical world where candy was so abundant, and as we chewed and chewed our stale Swedish Fish, I told stories about Bazooka gum wrapped in pink-sugared comics, Atomic Fireballs so hot I had to spit them into my sticky fingers to give my tongue a break, and a TV commercial where a red-suited man on a trapeze platform chewed his incredibly long-lasting Bit-O-Honey until the stands cleared.

The night of the Swedish Fish from the Plum Island store was just a regular night, like hundreds of regular nights, sitting around the table with the kids, and on this night, there was no big ceremony, no melting of red fish on a smoldering sage pile to smoke out any lingering smudges of my nightmares. Why waste good candy? Because we had nothing else for dessert, and because I didn't need to hang on anymore, we shared the souvenir candy I'd carried home, prying the gobs of sticky sugar from the grooves in our teeth with our tongues.

Henry, never one for delayed gratification, shoved all his fish in his mouth, cheeks bulging and eyes shining, while Ella, our gentle vegan, arranged the red fish in her own sense-making pattern and then nibbled them one by one, nose to tailfin, studying the curving gills, the seven letters disguised by bumpy scales. *Thank you for keeping her safe.* While we waited for Ella to finish eating, I snapped open the tin box, and Henry and I pushed our fingers into the coarse sand, making paths and changing contours. The brown grains tumbled, turning up chunks of white shell shining like bones.

And this is where the story ends this time, around a real table with a real dream for real children: I want Ella and Henry to know, always, that it's okay to tell the truth, to name names and make noise, no matter what. I want them to lay down shame and be brave. I want them to be willing to go back when they know there is something they need to see or set free or reclaim—and then I want them to remember that the way is forward. I want them, always, to let the giving and the taking in of love and sweetness lift them up.

I want them to feel light.

I want them to know they can fly without crashing.

THE SURPRISE BABY

On a bleak, dripping Saturday in October, nine months pregnant with my first baby, I wedged myself behind the wheel of our old sedan, drove to a home improvement store, and loaded my cart with Thompson's water sealer for the deck, concrete filler for the sidewalk, and an asphalt repair kit for the driveway. I did all this with no conscious awareness that it was suddenly vital for me to fill in and seal all the cracks and crannies.

There would be no fissures, nothing to fall through.

Step on a crack, break your mother's back. Step on a line, break your mother's spine.

After months of vomiting, bone-deep exhaustion, and precipitous weight gain; stroller shopping, onesie washing, and car seat installation; urinary tract infections, nose bleeds, and heart palpitations; blood tests, urine samples, and ultrasounds on sonography equipment advanced enough to give the portrait studios a run for their money, our countdown-to-baby clicked into the single digits.

I had officially stopped working, and soon my mother would arrive to cook and do laundry and rub my bloated feet. Phew. Maybe, just maybe, pregnancy was a temporary condition. Maybe I *wouldn't* be pregnant forever, I thought, lowering myself down onto the couch feeling smug. I was a trooper, a rock star, a genuine do-it-all modern woman. Informed by my new pregnancy-inspired knowledge of human physiology, I stretched out—no, not stretched, not in week thirty-nine—I *distributed my aching bulk* on my left side, despite the numb spot in that hip, to avoid

compression of the vena cava. For those of you who have never
been pregnant and therefore have never had the occasion to care
one way or the other, the vena cava is the large vein running just
to the right of the spine, and I was depending on it to drain the
sluggish blood from the lower half of my body: more oxygen for
baby, less swelling for me.

With my feet pulsating on a pillow near the head of my husband, Mark, likely I was explaining some feature of the gravid
circulatory system to him as he enjoyed a vodka tonic and I wet
down my dry tongue with a club soda that wasn't fooling me
with its jaunty lemon wedge. Poking the lemon with my finger,
I felt my smug feeling melting faster than the tinkling ice cubes
in Mark's delicious-looking cocktail. With my emotions shifting
like fast-falling Tetris squares, I was just settling back into feeling
elephantine and sorry for myself when Mark chuckled and tilted
his laptop for me to see this headline on the ABC News site:

Woman gives birth to "surprise" baby

So this twenty-seven-year-old woman in South Australia started
having "mysterious stomach pain" Tuesday afternoon at work—
she felt, she said, "a bit unwell and bloated." She went home to
sleep it off, and when she woke up in the morning, the "cramping
really intensified." And do you know what she did? She went to
the emergency room, and that very afternoon she gave birth to
a "healthy baby boy." In the past month or so she'd noticed her
belly was "a little hard," but she had no idea she was pregnant.

Now, how in the name of the goddess and all things fair and
right in this world was such a thing *possible*?

"Well," Mark said, tilting the monitor back and taking a long,
slurpy draw on the vodka tonic, "apparently you've been blowing
this whole pregnancy thing way out of proportion."

Eight pounds! That Australian woman gave birth to a healthy,
eight-pound baby boy in the thirty-seventh week of her pregnancy *without ever having known she was pregnant*. This was not

a teenager. This was a grown woman. According to the report, she laughed and said, "It makes you wonder where I was hiding it!" *Yes, Australian lady, it most certainly does make me wonder.* I was envious of this on so many levels, but I also smelled a rat. (Apparently, her husband had told her he was unable to father children because of a car accident. I wasn't sure how that played in, but I was quite certain it had.)

In the real world of pregnancy, the elastic in my Victoria's Secret bikini underwear—the largest size Victoria offers before even *she* knows the secret's out of the bag—had been wearing half-inch grooves into the abundant flesh on my hips, and I decided it was time to accept the fact that the supposedly sexy, under-the-belly style touted by the hip, young mama zines wasn't going to hack it for me anymore. In the maternity section at Meijer's—the same midwestern superstore where we buy ice cream bars and lawn fertilizer—I found the biggest underwear I had ever seen. The package read, "One size fits most."

Imagine my relief when I was one of the "most."

Two nights later, after a four a.m. trip to the bathroom, I was wide awake and obsessing about four things: white noise in the nursery, baby-appropriate cold vapor humidifiers, cervical ripeness as determined by a scale called the Bishop's Score (what was I, a peach?), and how we were supposed to be able to tell at home whether the baby was tolerating contractions well.

During my pregnancy I had scorned sushi and bleu cheese, swallowed folic acid and calcium, and stayed away from pubs, hot tubs, and beauty salons. I had counted trimesters, months, weeks, days, servings, pounds, kicks, calories, and contractions until I felt like a Montessori kid in the corner with her abacus— and still I worried. I worried about all that I couldn't see, and I looked so hard at those things I *could* see, everything from the requisite servings of leafy greens to the fascinating linea nigra drawing downward from my poking belly button, but I could not hang onto even the idea of an *actual baby*.

I felt as if I were missing something—like the subjects in that famous study who are instructed to watch a video and count the number of passes on a basketball court. So intense is their focus on the ball, on getting the count right, that a full 90 percent fail to notice the woman in the gorilla suit who runs out onto the court and pounds her chest for the camera.

Throughout my pregnancy, I swear, I tried to see the gorilla. With my eyes, I had seen the two blue lines in the pregnancy test window. In the dim room of my nightly sleeplessness, I could see my taut mountain of a belly. Technology had even allowed me a glimpse of my swimming baby projected in all her ultrasonographic glory, stretching her tiny fingers wide. Was that a wave? A flashed peace sign?

And yet, pregnancy was a hard concept for me to fully wrap my mind around: *In your body, Jill, you are growing a person. She began with the meeting of sperm and egg, a microscopic possibility, moved on from zygote to embryo to full-on fetus, and now she is seven or eight pounds, and she is a she, or so they say, and soon she will emerge from your body. Somehow in the next two weeks, she will be born—you will open up and push her out, or something will go wrong and they will cut her out, but one way or another she will be made separate from you, you will be two people, and she will be your daughter. She will have a name and live in your house. And you will love her more than you have ever loved anyone before.* These are some of the things I understood to be true of the biological endeavor in which I was presently engaged, but I was forced to leave much to faith. I had never had so much to lose, and yet, I didn't even know, really, what such a loss would mean, what I would be losing.

The fifth thing I was fretting over in those early morning hours was my recent jarring of the doctor-ordered "first urine of the morning" for my weekly appointment. I'd arrived at four a.m. somewhat arbitrarily, an averaging of morning urine, because

I could have collected at one a.m., or three, or later at six, but four seemed just about right. All that collecting and rinsing and bagging and storing had me pretty much wide awake: Had I done the right thing? Was this the right urine? Were the proteins and sugars in my urine at exactly four a.m. *representational* proteins and sugars? Or had I somehow skewed the sample? Were the glaring signs of baby-threatening preeclampsia or gestational diabetes lurking in the five a.m. urine only?

As dawn broke, my mind skittered around like a Mexican jumping bean warmed in a child's sticky palm, and after I moved on to wondering if I'd ever again compose a metaphor that was not somehow related to pregnancy, birth, babies, or children, I settled on this thought: the woman in Australia with the healthy eight-pound baby boy never jarred a single urine sample in the duration of her ostensibly unnoticed full-term pregnancy. How was this *possible*? Was there nothing to notice? Nothing to *see*?

Up long before the sun, I lay on my left side watching the ceiling fan whir in lazy circles and trying to imagine what it would be to approach birth and motherhood with absolutely no preparation. I don't mean the footie pajamas and the bouncy seats and the miniature padded bathtubs. I don't even mean the prenatal testing and physical exams. What I mean is the mental groundwork. For better or worse, not only did the Australian woman fail to see the chest-pounding ape, but she wasn't even watching the ball on the court. There was no court. She counted nothing. Prepared for nothing. For thirty-seven weeks, the duration of her full-term pregnancy, the only cue she permitted herself to process was that her belly was "a little hard." She must have been looking so far beyond her body that she somehow managed not to see the signs of her pregnancy.

It wasn't so different, I realized, from what I had been doing: analyzing urine, charting weight gain, smoothing thick cocoa butter on my stretched skin, diagnosing every ache and bulge.

This is not baby, I thought. *This is* pregnancy. *These are not the same.*

Where was my girl in her gorilla suit? I could not see her. No matter what I measured, she would surprise me. I would be surprised.

Squatting in the driveway the next day, I squeezed Kegels and used a weeding fork to pry stubborn dandelions from a long crack to make a clean run for the asphalt filler. We are not a species that abides a gap. Superstitions attached to the cracks and fissures I was so intent on filling abound, threatening more than just our mothers' spines—though surely my own was aching. For example, squashing an anthill rising up out of a crack might bring on the rains. The grass growing up in these open spaces could be a harbinger of a hard winter. Any of the cracks could make a doorway for spirits to fly in from the other side, and that seems to be the gist of it: we're all about compartmentalizing and dividing. I suspect this makes us feel safe—or safer. My world, your world. The earthly versus the spiritual. What is civilized and what is wild.

But already the borders had been ruptured, no? Inside my body was a creature I had helped to create—using a microscopic biological process outside my control and certainly beyond my comprehension. For months, I had been feeding this creature with my very blood, oxygenating her with the air I breathed, and—here's the kicker—*this creature was not me.* I get that this is the way it's done all over the world, but just take a moment to consider how mind-blowingly body breaching this is: we women grow new human beings in our bodies with the tacit understanding that we will nurture and protect these creatures until they are able to step over the threshold and walk away from us. *That's the plan,* I thought, down on my knees now, holding my weeding fork like an ancient spear and really going at a particularly gaping crack.

What was I doing? Really? Was I trying to protect myself from all that might sneak through to get us, or worse, the possibility of slipping through into something I couldn't see on the other side? I wondered about my Australian counterpart, she who had shared pregnancy with me, week by week, never knowing. What were she and her infant son doing now? What would *I* do when my own baby arrived? What kind of sea change did motherhood have in store for me, and more, who would my baby be after she crossed the border of my body? How would I know where I stopped and she began? Maybe we wouldn't. Maybe the space between us wouldn't look like a crack to be filled in but something more like water or blood or air, a space we could move through without feeling the jolt of the crossing, or even the bump of the seam.

That's what I want, I thought, finishing with the last crack and easing onto my feet, straightening up to get a good look at my work. Mark would fill in the gaps later so the baby and I wouldn't breathe any fumes. *I want this baby, whoever she is. I want the love we can never see but know is there.*

THE RIVER CAVE

In my twenties, many years before my daughter was born, I had a question: In a crazy, dangerous world where wars are fought and children are neglected and starving, in a world where six-year-olds are raped and dogs are abandoned in paper bags on highways, in a world where young women want so desperately to be thin they stick their fingers down their throats to purge all that is wrong and bad—in a world like this, *can I really have a baby?*

This was a complicated question.

Now the answer is flesh, down in the yard playing in the sandbox with her grandmother, my mother, a woman who has made a lot of mistakes, yes, but who has always loved me. I can hear her now through the open window chattering with my eighteen-month-old daughter about shovels and trains and the tweeting of birds. She loved me, and now she loves my baby and my baby loves her.

There's a twenty-five-pound girl sitting in the yard measuring sand and counting rocks because I carried her in my body, gave birth to her, and held her close to my breast until she learned to take a few steps away from me and then a few more. Ahead of us is this whole life that she is going to have separate and apart from me.

Down in the yard, this life is already happening. So now I have a new question, don't I?

Now what?

Now she is here, and she is no longer a baby who needs to be imagined but is herself, Ella, a kid who likes apple juice in a box and the model train circling above the frozen food section of our grocery store, a kid who counts to eleven and loves the alphabet song but can only remember A-B-C, P, T-U-V, and Z. That's today. Tomorrow will be different. Up until two days ago, she took a nap at noon, easily, and now, no nap. No. She's onto something new, and her father and I are scrabbling to keep up.

How will we keep her safe and still allow her to live a good life? How do we teach her about the value of love with our actions and then try to explain what constitutes a "bad touch," even from someone we know? Maybe someone we've asked her to hug? Don't we want our babies to live in a circle of affection?

What about the thrill of adventure and the richness of new experiences? On a boat, I think of drowning. On a horse, I replay the story of my mother's friend's child who was dragged to death by the hired pony at his sixth birthday party.

What about daycare and school and birthday parties? Ella has a life-threatening reaction to milk—if she consumes any dairy her throat swells and she cannot breathe. Having witnessed this, how do I turn my eyes away from her mouth and every morsel that goes into it? How do I let her hold hands at circle time with a kid fresh from a bag of cheesy snacks? I cannot. And I must.

As parents, we can harbor fairly reasonable fears about everything from grapes and hot dogs (choking) to toilets and mop buckets (drowning)—and this is before we move beyond the relative safety of our particular domestic situation and into the world of drunks driving fast cars and pedophiles waiting at bus stops.

I am afraid and I am ashamed. My daughter drinks clean water; plays in a safe, fenced yard; and receives regular medical care. Here there are no suicide bombers or child soldiers. How do parents in, say, the West Bank send their children out to school? I'm sure some don't, and the rest—knowing they must, knowing that life demands living no matter the circumstances—must feel as though they are helping to tie shoes on their own hearts, just cut from their bleeding bodies. Run, heart, run.

How do they do it? I do not know.

Ella has grown bored with the sandbox, and she and my mother are now circling the yard, stopping to smell flowers. "Go away, bee!" I hear Ella shout. "Go away!" I stand to take a look, and from two stories up I cannot see any bees. My mother takes Ella's hand and assures her that she is fine. The bee is an ant. She is safe.

Now what? This is not just one question.

I am fearful. I know this about myself.

When Ella was a scrap of a human in her stroller, I remember being on a walk together when an old woman seemed to aim her car at us. The car was moving slowly, and I knew we were never in any real danger. I could have outrun that car and kept us both safe, but all I had to do was turn the stroller up onto a lawn. My evasive action snapped the woman out of her daze: *Baby*, she must have been thinking. *Baby.* As my driver's ed teacher always warned, when you fixate on something, a person or an accident, you steer toward it. That's just what happens, and so the woman was coming at us, thinking about the baby, probably thinking how she mustn't, mustn't *hit* the baby, and when she saw the baby's mother scamper onto the lawn, she swerved away, all the way across the street and into the other lane, one hand fluttering in the air like a broken bird. We were in the path of her car for only a few moments, but they played out in slow motion, and there was plenty of time for my mother-brain to rehearse: I would have flung Ella out of danger with a burst of strength. I would die for her. Of course I would. But my brain didn't stop there. I worked it out further into the future: a neighbor would find the unharmed baby, make sure she got home to her father, who would need to remarry posthaste so that my baby would not be a motherless child.

This is the way my brain works in a few seconds. Imagine the grim scenarios I can construct given the luxury of a whole day. For the most part, I've wriggled free of my worst crazies, exorcised the most hideous of demons, but this one insidious trick of the brain remains: to a pathological degree, I fear the death of those I love. No one knows why this is exactly, and each of my six former therapists resigned themselves to leaving this protective mechanism in place since I'm able to function "normally."

Perhaps the fear took root in the sexual abuse of my childhood—not an obvious connection, but once, having diagnosed me with posttraumatic stress disorder, a therapist made that link. I have other symptoms of PTSD, more benign. For example, if you love me, you learn quickly that it's not fun or funny to hide in a broom closet and jump out to surprise me. First, I will scream a scream that will singe your hair, and then I will crumple to the floor in a pile of frayed nerve endings and sob. Sudden, loud noises take their toll. The Fourth of July sends me under the bed with the dog. So that's a possibility, but I can't remember how far this fear goes back.

When did I start being afraid of everyone I love dying?

When I was twenty, my fiancé was riding home from work one night in a white Chrysler minivan with his coworkers from Virgin Lightships in Tillamook, Oregon, when their vehicle was broadsided by a tow truck going highway speed. It seems that the driver of Colin's van failed to obey the stop sign, failed to yield in any way, and drove into the path of the truck without a flicker of a brake light.

Here again, there are more questions than answers. Aren't there always when someone we love dies?

Why didn't the driver brake? Was he checking traffic in the wrong direction because he was British? But then, on a two-lane highway, wouldn't it be necessary to look both ways? Were the brakes faulty in some way the investigators missed? Did he smash down the pedal and get only mush? Or maybe the truck startled him and in his urgency he missed the pedal? Or, the worst, was he playing chicken with the tow truck? With a vanload of twenty-something young men as his audience, did he think he could make it to the other side before the truck got to them? Did his bravado outweigh caution? If he had made it, if the tow truck driver had laid on his horn and glared at the stupid boys in the white van as it flashed away into the darkness, if Colin had turned his head to look behind, one arm thrown casually over the back of the bench seat, and said, "Man, you idiot, that was a close one," maybe even in an admiring way, and then turned back to the front, laughing with his three friends, that would have been that: a moment forgotten, never mentioned, nothing.

But that's not what happened. Another thing of an infinite number of options happened. Colin's head was crushed. They wouldn't even let me see him. The driver and the man sitting beside him both died. There was one survivor, another young man, this one from Michigan, also engaged to be married. He was sitting next to Colin, and he lived. Sometimes I think about this man and his wife. I wonder if their lives took a path resembling the one they'd envisioned before that night. I doubt it.

I know this is not revelatory. I know this is how accidents happen: suddenly, randomly, crushingly. But in the slow months after the accident, my heart took in this knowledge like a sea change: I could love a breathing someone, and then, like that, he could be gone.

Even writing this catches my breath. I have to concentrate to keep my heart pumping in my chest. My baby is safe. By now she's trundled into the house trailing her Grammy. She's eating Cheerios, nobody's known choking hazard, drinking some juice, double-strapped into her booster chair, watching *Sesame Street*. To counteract any bad thoughts, the possible power of my own imagination, I perform a mental exercise the mother of my river-running boyfriend taught to me: I picture my baby in a golden bubble. She is munching happily, tapping her foot to the music. The bubble protects her through the power of visualization, and even when I'm not in the room, I help to keep her safe.

I was not a protected child—loved, and loved dearly, but not pro-tected. My mother trusted us to take care of ourselves, and it should be said that she didn't have a lot of choice in the matter. My mother left my father when I was two, driving north from Miami in a van and ending up on the coast of Massachusetts with two kids and no money. As my mother rightly points out, the climate was different back then. There was not so much fear. My mother exposed us to the world and let us learn. We were the last house before a nature preserve on a little island, and thus I knew the pleasure of being a child left alone to wander through sand dunes. I gathered wheaty beach grasses into bouquets and toasted them in the sun; I dug out a spot for myself in the warm sand near a pungent bayberry bush and read *The Black Stallion* straight through in one glorious afternoon; I poked a branch into the sticky nests hanging from the trees and pulled it back dangling with fuzzy caterpillars like a prize.

But we know the problem with this picture. The world is a dangerous place, and an unsupervised child is an at-risk child. My mother has no reason to feel bad: her two kids are grown, employed, artistic, happy, and happily married, each to partners they actually love, each with children they really love—all in all, they're pretty all right. My mother, working mostly alone, did not fail us.

That needs to be said—and then it needs to be repeated that my brother and I were often and largely unprotected. Between the ages of six and twelve, I was molested by a neighbor. My mother never knew. Between the ages of thirteen and nineteen, I inflicted abuses upon myself: relentless bulimia, blackout drinking, cutting, risky sex. She never knew. Again, I want to defend her: I never told her, right? I did everything I could to appear normal. I was not a difficult child or even a defiant teenager. I wanted to be good, and good enough. I wanted her to love me. I was the teenage girl who would break a mother's heart, but I didn't want my mother's heart to break, and so I was another teenager as well, the one my mother chose to see.

In the end, I turned out all right. Maybe better than all right.

And now I'm a mother with a daughter of my own.

I can read parenting manuals until Dr. Spock rises from the dead and becomes a born-again proponent of the family bed, and I won't find what I'm looking for in those pages. As ever, the questions are complicated and varied.

Does good parenting make a good kid? What constitutes good parenting? Just the right balance of protection and freedom? What's a good kid? One who complies with our wishes? Does her chores and gets good grades and smiles easily when we ask it of her? What if that same kid is crawling out the casement windows at night, drinking and drugging and sexing it up? What if her parents never even know, and in her adulthood all that irons out? What if that good baby turned bad kid turns again and becomes a quality citizen who gets dutifully in her car each morning, stops at the drive-thru espresso joint for a coffee, pays her mortgage and the monthly payment on that car, participates in all that our capitalist society has to offer? Is that what we're hoping for? Or is a good kid the one who knows her way around a serious set of choices? A kid who rebels once in a while because she has a stable sense of self and knows what she wants and needs from this world? And do good kids always become good adults, and what exactly is a good adult? What's our goal here? Happiness? Social conscience? Kindness? *Breath?*

After Colin's death, it took me a while to rediscover fear. I remember a feeling of great and mournful recklessness.

I tempted fate.

And so one afternoon about four months after the accident, I found myself at the mouth of a cave with two companions: Colin's brother and a woman whose brother had also died violently in the last year. We were a ragged and wounded team, and we were traveling through Central America together. The cave was in central Guatemala, and our guide was a ten-year-old boy who wouldn't go into the cave, no.

Here's a thing about me fifteen years later: I would *never* go into this cave now. But back then, I don't remember that we hesitated, even when our guide stopped at the mouth, sat on a rock, gestured into the wet blackness, and shook his head no, no, not me: *muy peligroso.*

Starting out, we had three flashlights between us, but happily, we heeded the advice of the German back at the *finca* and also brought candles; we lit them, sticking the candles to the cliff walls here and there with melted wax as we headed in. This place was scary. Bats everywhere—hanging shadows, diving specters. Guatemala is one of those countries *vampire* bats still call home. I don't remember caring.

At one point the channel got so narrow that the cave ceiling came down to meet the water—did I mention that most of our mile-long journey was done waist-deep in a moving river? A *cave* river? We had to swim *under* the water. But I don't remember feeling afraid. Now, thinking about how I plunged my head, my whole self, into the flooded, mysterious darkness cognizant of the possibility that I would find rock and not air on the other side . . . well, I am sickened. Before going under, I do think we hesitated—clearly, this was folly—but the German (was it the German again?) had told us about this low point in the cave. He had told us it would open up again on the other side. We had known the German for one day. We dove under.

Moving into this cave in my memory is like moving into memory itself, and at the point where the last of our three flashlights sputtered and expired, I want to say we were at a place where we would have been forced to turn back anyway. I want to say that we were standing at the top of an underground waterfall, but I can't conjure a clear vision, and wouldn't such a natural wonder burn its image on my brain? Or perhaps my brain was too clouded by grief. I do remember the journey back because I felt a shiver of fear, and I welcomed the unfamiliar prickle. I didn't want to die in this watery cave and I was glad.

We were in near total blackness, and returning to the mouth of the cave meant feeling our way along the sharp edges of the walls and hoping we hadn't missed any branching channels, hoping the flickering light from our next melting candle would scatter off the swooping walls, a sparkle, a glint, but enough to lead us back to the cautious boy holding our sandwiches. Stupid Americans.

The hike back to the *finca* took us through a banana grove with drooping leaves large enough to make a hammock for a baby. I remember feeling good to be out in the sunshine again after so much darkness and only a sputtering of light.

That night I got sick, the most wrenching sickness of the whole journey. That was strange because we were at a ranch run by North Americans, and there had been much talk about the safe and delicious food.

The place was poison. I spent the night on my knees in the grass outside our bunkhouse, feeling far, far away from home and, yes, wanting my mother. I wanted my mother to hold my hair and rub my back. I wanted ginger ale and saltines. I wanted to go home. A large iguana stood on top of a ragged fence post letting his tail drape dramatically down toward the too-green grass. He rotated his eyes with a tick-tick of full vision. Googly eyes. This guy could look anywhere he wanted, but he trained both eyeballs on me.

I was on my back in the dankly warm grass, sharing my resting place with God knows what in this false fairy tale of tropical foliage jacked up by modern fertilizers. That morning, before the journey to the cave, I'd been chased by two giant parrots, ripping rainbows of birds, screaming down from the treetops and skimming my ponytail with their wingtips. "I was jogging," I told the iguana, delirious with fever and puking. "I bet you know them. Around here, probably nobody runs unless they're running *from* something, huh?" I was in Dr. Doolittle land, stuck in the glossy illustrations at the center of the book, talking in full, dawning color to an enormous green lizard on a brown post in a green, green world. He seemed to understand. His world was changing too.

"I want to go home," I told him.

If this were fiction, perhaps I could present that day and night in Guatemala as the apex of my fearlessness, wading into that bat-hung cave, lying in the grass with my large lizard friend— shouldn't *I* have been afraid of *him*? But this is not fiction, and certainly there were other moments of both recklessness and jolting caution to litter the narrative path winding toward the paralyzing fear of new motherhood.

Fifteen years ago I walked into a cave and surprised myself by being happy to return to the sun. Telling the story of the river cave, I want the light to sparkle at the top of the metaphor. I want to pronounce loudly that I will not raise my daughter to live inside my fear for her. That sounds wonderful, but I have no idea what such a proclamation would mean in actual practice. When I think of Ella going so far from home, plunging her head into the murky wet, all those bats, my God, my heart clenches, but what if she *wants* to go into a dark, subtropical cave, real or metaphorical? I do not know. Instead, perhaps, I can find evidence here for a choice to be made—the choice to set up a family camp at the mouth of the cave with the boy holding the sandwiches, the choice to live in the light together.

Would that work? Or do I have to *be* the boy with the sand-wiches? Do I wait on the rock in the light gripping the rolled top of the brown paper bag in my sweating hands, waiting for Ella to come back and eat with me?

After Colin died and before my trip, I had moved back home and my mother kept me alive—she fed and sheltered and loved me.

In the beginning, when I was physically incapacitated by grief, she even bathed me. A couple of months later, I realized I had to leave. The same meticulous mother-care that had sustained me was starting to disable me. I didn't need to live for myself because she was doing it for me.

My mother tells me that taking me to the airport and watching me get on a plane to San Jose, Costa Rica, was one of the hardest things she has ever done. She remembers following me as far as she could—past check-in, through security, all the way to the mouth of the gangway. How fragile I must have looked to her, a twenty-year-old daughter, numb and glassy-eyed with grief, reeling from the world's turning, made small again by this new knowledge of death. How much must I have looked like her baby tottering toward the edge of the stairs, a cliff. She tells me now that she wanted to hold onto me. She wanted to go with me.

But she said nothing. Instead, she helped me hoist my backpack onto my bent shoulders and checked the straps on the rolled sleeping sheet she'd sewn to protect me from dirty beds. Then she let me go. She cradled her leather pocketbook and watched me stumble down the gangway. I turned at the bottom and blew her a kiss. *Bye Mom bye.*

During a time when I didn't have the capacity to carry my own fear, my mother loved me enough not to give me hers to hold instead. Three months later I came back to her with a story about a river cave and a talking iguana. Fifteen more years and I'm back again. This time I've brought Ella, another chance, and I'm ready to tell the story of the cave again.

The bats! My God, the bats were everywhere.

BIRD GIRLS

I wake up, a wife and mother, at five a.m. on a July morning in the middle of Indiana, not because my baby cries or my husband snores but because the birds are going wild. Early bird nothing. They're *all* early—and their racket shakes memory down from the maple trees in my mortgaged backyard like seeds from a feeder hit by a marauding squirrel. Everything shivers and trills. I'm in a Proustian moment, fifteen years ago, zipped into a tent with my then-boyfriend Stevie, listening to this same cacophony of whistles and peeps, breathing in the smell of woodsmoke and coffee.

It's still dark on a late spring morning in Oregon, not much past four, and the professor of Stevie's birding class is about to take us on a trek through the woods. I know nothing about birds. Ignorant and cold, I shrug into the requisite Patagonia fleece jacket, duck through the nylon flap at the front of the tent, and join the others following the bearded ornithologist into the dawning forest.

Soft stepping over brown needles, he is our Pied Piper and we his captivated children. When he hears a particular bird noise, he holds his hand up to halt us, twenty or so bleary-eyed college students. Pointing to his ear, then to the source of the sound— sometimes visible, more often not—Bird Man whispers the name of the singer to us: Hammond's flycatcher, lesser goldfinch, mountain chickadee, American dipper, bushtit. Stevie and the other students scribble these names down in birding notebooks. I listen, impressed, and shuffle along behind the group.

I cheated just now with the names, of course, although I remember *bushtit* and *flycatcher* and also seeing the spellings of the bird sounds—*pzrrt, pip-pip, treip*—and thinking, *Huh. Bird words.* (Stevie majored in biology; I didn't wander far from the English department.) I remember riding in a university van to our campsite, and I remember that early morning walk, but the thing that wedges in my brain between *bushtit* and *pip-pip* is the sticky feeling that I didn't belong, the black-tar goo of old insecurity.

I wasn't in the class. I was a girlfriend tag-a-long, but there was more to it than that. I was the prissy one. I was too much lipstick and not enough crunch. All of Stevie's bird class friends were of the outdoorsier-than-thou category, and I had brought along an inflatable sleeping pad and tiny jar of half-and-half for my coffee. I can't remember anybody ever *saying* anything, just this sense that somehow I had been mismatched with my dreadlocked, kayak-paddling, pottery-throwing, Teva-wearing boyfriend. I felt girly in a bad way, as if my painted toenails and snug jeans were a romantic liability—no, worse, an *identity* liability.

My love of birds hadn't brought me to that twittering Oregon glen: Stevie had to be watched. My adversaries were young women in tie-dyed shirts, hemp bracelets, and baggy cargo pants, pockets stuffed with hand-blown pipes and big-bellied goddess figurines, and I wanted to say, *You know what? You want outdoorsy? You want to know hippie chick? When I was a teenager I lived on a mountain in a plastic house, okay? I rode a horse to school. We weren't camping. That was how we lived. Yeah, I shaved my armpits, but I melted snow in a bucket on the woodstove to do it.*

This was all true. I had come to appreciate the pleasure of a soft bed and creamy coffee the hard, cold way when I was thirteen and my mother packed all our worldly belongings into a Chevy pickup, tied them down with fishing twine, and moved us to a mountaintop in northeastern Washington. We were so far off the grid that in the winter when the roads were impassable we pulled orange sleds loaded with our groceries and clean laundry the last two miles home with ropes around our waists like pack animals. My mother claimed this was the kind of activity that built character, but another lasting effect of those frigid hikes was my reduced tolerance for those who thought a weekend in the woods was roughing it.

Stevie knew my mountain-girl history, of course, but I felt I needed to remind him of the tough girl that lurked beneath my feminine exterior. I wanted him to know that I could feather a soft nest and still hold off the egg-snatchers with my piercing beak. Or something like that. Maybe I missed the day in biology class where we learned that the females choose the males in the bird world. The males are the pretty ones. Think peacocks. Think the blue bowerbird posing on his well-decorated threshold. In retrospect, some careful consideration of the actual facts might have saved me a few proprietary predawn treks into the trilling woods. But like those of the Bird Girls, and like Stevie's, mine was an identity in the process of becoming, and we were all involved in the awkward process of molting and feathering, craning our necks to check out our butts and see how our plumes were shaping up.

With more than a little shame, I recognize that the lessons I'd been learning in Women's Studies 101 about the patriarchy perpetuating woman-to-woman competition hadn't exactly sunk in. The Bird Girls weren't my only rivals, and they certainly weren't the crunchiest. The Ceramics Girls got dirtier, the Ultimate Frisbee Girls ran faster, the Kayak Girls, well, the Kayak Girls were tough—even I gave them that.

I tried to be the girl Stevie could love. I listened for birds in the woods, I straddled the pottery wheel and let it spray my jeans with clay juice, and I developed a mean forehand on the Ultimate field. I even paddled a small plastic boat into crushing rapids and thanked all the appropriate earth goddesses that I'd been born bottom-heavy and therefore managed to roll back up to breathe again. But I never *felt* tough. Worse, I never felt like the girl I was pretending to be.

You know how this story ends. Not long after the bird trip, Stevie moved out, and when he left, as I had predicted, he paired up with one of those gritty girls. Her name was also Jill. This new Jill was everything that I was not: the anti-Jill Jill. In one of those too-honest, unnecessarily painful post-breakup conversations, Stevie confessed that he'd felt smothered by my girliness—with me, he said, there was "too much feminine energy."

A couple of months after we broke up, Other Jill approached me on campus—baggy pants splattered with mud, shaggy hair not unattractively mussed, square hands holding a rope leash attached to a giant, drooling St. Bernard. She asked me if I'd seen Stevie. He hadn't called in weeks, she said. Unsuccessfully, I fought the urge to feel pleased.

I shrugged. "Nope, haven't seen him."

Poor Jill.

Where are you, Bird Girls, on this dawning Indiana day? The raucous songs of morning send me back to you, fifteen years and two thousand miles away. Settled, finally, in a nest I know to be mine, do I miss the parts of me that were you in those restless years of feathering and refeathering? Of never really landing?

Where are you, Bird Girls? Are you still sleeping? Perhaps you're lying awake, like me, remembering walks in the woods with birds and boys, all long gone. Maybe you're already up or haven't yet slept—rocking babies, typing reports, finishing shifts.

On this morning in Indiana, the sun colors the sky pink, and my baby girl rolls over in her sleep. Having learned to hear my daughter's every shift and sigh, I know how I could have behaved on that forest path, tuning my ears rather than my jealous eyes. On the sidewalk with the sad-eyed Jill, I might have said, "No, I haven't seen him. But it isn't you, you know. You're okay just the way you are." But I didn't, and of course, I couldn't. Sometimes we take our whole lives to feel safe in our nests; sometimes we miss that chance entirely. I am lucky.

Hey, Bird Girls, where are you now? Mine was a failure of empathy—for you and for myself. Where are you?

I am here.

Hello out there. *Pzrrt. Pip-pip.*

LIFE'S NOT A PARAGRAPH

I am married to a poet. Once, bemoaning the fact that so many of my husband, Mark's, poems feature his old girlfriend, fixed in the sharp beauty and cold fury of her midtwenties, captivating even to me in her perfect unattainability, never aging, I said, "Why don't you ever write any poems about me?" Mark shrugged: "Try breaking up with me. Then you'd get some poems."

In a break-up story or the-one-who-got-away tale of woe, it's all there—tension and betrayal, disappointment and decline, fighting and fucking, all that exquisite heartbreak. But what if the heart stays intact? What then? Do we take the story back to the beginning? Way back to the unlikely conception and birth of our heroine?

Once upon a time, a long, long time ago, in a land far, far away, a baby girl was born into the dragon-breath heat of a south Florida summer, arriving too late for the summer of love but crowning just as Janis Joplin was busting out with "Piece of My Heart" on a rain-soaked stage in Woodstock, New York. The day was August 16, 1969. As birth stories go, I'll take it.

My poor mother missed the whole thing—my birth, not Janis, although her, too—because those were the days of twilight sleep, and my mother's memories were not given the opportunity to lay down tracks. She was there—and likely conscious, if a little loopy—but the twilight cocktail wiped the story clean. Drugged by the doctors who pulled me into the light, my mother would have lingered in the crepuscular in-between before her memories fell into darkness. Maybe she got to hold me, count toes, kiss my fingers, but likely not. What efficient doctor would take the time for that? In 1969 the Miami Baby Hospital was not in the business of love, bonding, and the making of memories. "My greatest regret," my mother says over forty years later, "is that I was not awake when you kids were born."

My father's no help in filling in the missing details because when the contractions fell into a pattern, he dropped my mother off at the hospital and headed out with my four-year-old brother, Ian, to hang over the safety rail and watch Cookie, the largest crocodile in captivity, snap up live chickens at feeding time. Think of the crashing jaws, flying feathers, and gore! Imagine how this scene may have mirrored whatever unremembered things were going on at the baby hospital. Eek.

Thus I was born, but that wasn't really the beginning of this story. My father remembers that he was supposed to be at Woodstock and for the very good reason that he'd been commissioned to do some sculptures for the venue; the plan had been that he would personally transport the art in a van. Because the original due date for my birth was July 4, nobody thought there would be any problem with the trip. If all went as planned, I'd be six weeks old by the time Woodstock rolled around. But all did *not* go as planned. Somehow, I arrived six weeks late. Throughout my childhood, I believed this story as the convenient genesis tale at the root of my chronic lateness, but now that I've been pregnant a few times myself, I know that *no* baby is six weeks late. Doesn't happen. When I challenge my mother on this detail, she sticks with her story. She *knows* I was supposed to arrive on the Fourth of July, at which point in the conversation she brings up the tumor and another somewhat suspect series of medical events.

According to my mother, her abdomen had spawned a tumor the size of a grapefruit—*a grapefruit!*—and so she was *on the table* being prepped for surgery when it was determined that the tumor had shrunk to nothingness. The tumor was gone, and lo, it had been replaced by a thickening womb. A child, not a grapefruit. Whether there was sonography equipment involved or an actual scalpel is anyone's guess after all these years. As a child, when I would hear this story, I'd feel a shudder of relief: but for the grace of God, right? I could have been mistaken for a tumor and surgically removed—and because of the tumor-as-grapefruit metaphor (never a softball or a newborn's head), I'd imagine the abortion being performed with the curved, serrated blade of a grapefruit knife. Shiver.

This is the human condition: pre-conception, conception, gestation, birth, and after-birth (which is to say, *life*) present so many opportunities for chance and error in even the most controlled environment. And what environment ruled by the vicissitudes of love and sex, or even just one egg and one sperm among the millions, is controlled? For any of us to emerge from the fluid darkness of the womb to suck in a phlegmy breath of actual air and release that first lusty cry—what are the *chances*?

I could so easily be someone else entirely, as could Mark, and all the rest up and down the family line to the miraculous children we named and call ours. If one second changes, one solitary moment, one single instant, we imagine ourselves out of existence.

Thinking about the improbability of our own beginning is almost as bad as thinking about the certainty of the end. I don't know how we all live with it.

I was born of a planned pregnancy, in a manner of speaking. Both my parents are artists. They met at the Rhode Island School of Design in the early sixties. I don't know the story of their actual meeting beyond a vague sense that they were introduced at a party, and that the party may actually have been thrown by Grammy Sarah, my father's mother, who was also an artist and had a house on Martha's Vineyard everyone called "The Barn" in addition to her apartment in the Bronx, where she owned a funky antique shop near the zoo. Grammy Sarah was an eccentric, more handsome than beautiful, but intellectual and worldly and *wild*. She was a single mother with panache—my father was born as the result of a shipside affair during World War II—but she was also a drinker. A dangerous, difficult, extravagant mother who lived large.

In contrast, my mother grew up in another kind of alcoholic home where shades were drawn tight and secrets locked down. Her father was a well-respected high school principal who stowed backup Budweiser tallboys in the deep pockets of suit jackets that hung like condemned men in his closet. My grandmother, the school librarian, big-hearted and gregarious by nature, knew enough to keep her finger to her lips and her distance at home, preferring to stay in the kitchen, watch her tiny TV, chain smoke, and read mysteries—none of which shed light on the dark marriage in which she'd landed. At 6 p.m. precisely, after the saying of grace (*Grant-us-thy-blessing-oh-heavenly-father-for-what-we-are-about-to-receive*) and the passing of the softened butter in the covered glass dish, there was no talking at my young mother's family table—just the clink and ping of knives and forks on china.

On the other hand, my mother tells me, Grammy Sarah's parties were "the best on the Vineyard." These parties, where people drank burgundy out of jars, swirled batik scarves and skirts in the dancing light of the well-stoked fire, and talked over the live music about art were a wonder to my teenaged mother. The Barn was open-concept living before that was a thing: the whole first floor was a kitchen–living room–entertaining space featuring "a concrete floor with pillows and candles and flowers everywhere." There was enough food and drink for all comers. My dad came from the kind of drinking family that knew how to party.

"I may have been more enamored of Grammy Sarah than I was of your father," my mother has told me, and I believe her because we all pretty much felt that way about Sarah. To know her was to love her, or at least be drawn to fly into her flame, to dive into the cyclonic swirl of her excess, to drink of the poison she proffered in the sparkling glass. Sarah and my father's father were never married, and her marriage to the man who was my father's stepfather and from whom we take our family name was brief and broken. She was not the marrying type.

I can see how my young mother would have fallen under her spell. Grammy Sarah herself—not my father—presented my mother with an engagement ring.

Once, in grad school, my teacher scrawled a note onto a draft of one of my stories: *No story of conception is a pretty one.* I forget the story and the reason, but the phrase has stuck with me over the years, gaining mass like a tumbling dung beetle.

After the parties on the Vineyard, the diamond ring, and a first baby who was not me, my parents' marriage was dealt a death blow. On July 22, 1966, my thirteen-month-old brother toddled into the bathroom while my mother served that night's fish special in a downtown eatery and my father chatted with Grammy Sarah on the phone. My father didn't realize my brother was not in the room until he heard the scream from the bathroom. I have always wondered if Grammy Sarah was still on the other end of the line, listening to her only child's world unravel. In this moment of inattention and accident, all her plans for her only son's future with the pretty artist from Fishkill, New York, were undone, obliterated.

When my father got to the bathroom, Ian was still standing, the too-hot water from the shower hissing from the steaming faucet. My father reached into the scalding stream, grabbed the baby, and Ian's skin came off in his hands like the fuzz slides from a blanched peach. I have written this scene before. I am sick for all of them. Depending on what family story I am telling, the horrifying scene with the burning baby can serve as the beginning, the middle, or the end. In this, the narrative strand of my parents' marriage, the poor baby glows red at the top of the pyramid, the climax, the moment after which nothing is ever the same again.

The doctors gave my brother a 1 in 10 chance of survival. Ten percent. I have read that the widely believed statistic of an 80 percent divorce rate among parents who lose a child is a myth—way too high. But my brother didn't die. And my mother says she never blamed my father. Nevertheless, my parents' marriage faltered, and three months after the burning, my father moved to Syracuse, New York, for grad school and my mother stayed behind, renting a room near the hospital, waiting while my brother's skin healed, while he formed a new boundary between himself and the world. At this point, my own chances of moving from ovum to embryo were darn slim, but in the holiday season of 1968, my mother got sentimental, and in this way, I may owe a debt of gratitude to the oddly sensual perfume of sugar cookies coming out of the oven. Hot now. "It was the holidays!" my mother explains. She wanted a real family for my brother, and that desire led her to the next, and to me: "I wanted a baby that *matched*."

Like a lot of things my mother reports about some major life decisions, this statement sounds absurd at first. *A baby that matched?!* But think of the advantages and possibilities and the alternatives. If you're a young woman of twenty-five with a degree from an art college, a job waiting tables, a scarred but vibrant preschooler, plenty of beaus but no one you love with anything approaching the passion you carry for your son—and you've never actually filed for divorce from the absent but essentially amiable father of that much-adored boy—why wouldn't you go back for another? If what you *want* is another child to love alongside the first, and the first child is as bright and beautiful as seems reasonable to hope, why *not* dip back into the same spermic pool? If we think of the worst-case scenario, another separation and a divorce, why not simplify life with one meager child support check for *both* children, the *same* house in Connecticut for summer vacations with Dad?

Vanilla and yeast, both, are known aphrodisiacs.

PART I

Mark and I are writing in a loft at my mom's house in Washington, and I'm feeling the need to indulge in a brief meta departure. The kids are at the park with their grandmother. It's too fucking hot, so Mark's writing in his underwear, his clicking laptop warming the family jewels.

"What are you doing?" he asks, cocking an eyebrow toward the big chair where I sit in my own underwear with my own laptop. In this way, we are simpatico. I stand up and touch the slanting ceiling, arching my back into a deep stretch.

"Sexercise?" Mark asks hopefully.

I ignore him. "I'm trying to write a love story," I say. "It's hard."

"If you're going to write a love story, it has to have some dirty bits," Mark says, pulling me down onto the bed. "Otherwise nobody cares. Otherwise it's just a couple of dorks holding hands." He rolls on top of me and lifts my left leg by the ankle. "Do you want me to be your muse?"

I do.

Wait. Okay. Hold on. Let me try again.

Once upon a time, a long, long time ago, in a strange southern land swathed with kudzu and irrigated with bourbon and blood, there lived a beautiful young woman whose heart had been broken so many times—death, disaster, and, most recently, bitter betrayal—that she'd settled into a relationship with a good man, a kind man, whom she loved for his kindness but could never really *love*.

And then one day a stranger came to town, and it was the young woman's job as the graduate assistant in the Creative Writing Program at the University of Alabama to fetch the stranger at the airport and extend all manner of gracious hospitality.

On the drive, the young woman is amazed and delighted by how friendly and normal the stranger is—for being such a fancy poet—and by the time they make it to the hotel in Tuscaloosa, the poet feels comfortable enough to tell the younger woman she needs a tampon, and oh, fortuitous day, the younger woman happens to have a few swimming around with the pens and the lipsticks in the bottom of her purse. Later that night, our protagonist, a fiction writer, is stunned by the gruesome beauty of a poem the visitor reads about a slain goat's heart singing sweetly from its hanging head.

Before the end of the stranger's visit, the stranger is no longer a stranger—the tampons, the poems, the long conversations in the car. They are like sisters. The decapitated goat's name is Broken Thorn Sweet Blackberry, and his song "is sweet. The heart dies of this sweetness." The young woman knows now, with certainty, that she mustn't live without true love.

Finis.

But not the end, because when the poet returns to the University of Illinois, a floppy-haired aspiring poet stops by to ask her to write a letter of recommendation. She listens and nods as the aspiring poet, one Mark Neely, lists the programs to which he has applied—George Mason, Virginia Commonwealth, etcetera—and then she tells him she's *just* gotten back from doing a reading at the University of Alabama. Why hasn't he applied *there*?

He's not sure, he just didn't think to do it. "Alabama?"

"They're the nicest people," she tells him. And: "The students are so happy."

Life doesn't come with plot, but sometimes, for real, truth is stranger than fiction.

So our unlikely matchmaker sent the handsome young poet off to make one last hasty application. He got in with a fellowship, and since his long-time, live-in girlfriend had a library science degree and could secure employment in nearly any college town, he accepted the offer and moved south.

And still—beyond our respective mates—there is something else standing in the way of a love story to tell our children: I'm finished with coursework. I don't need any more classes, so I don't sign up for any. But when the news comes that novelist John Keeble will be returning to Tuscaloosa in the fall to teach just one graduate class—in the sprung novel—I decide to audit.

There was no funny business that semester, but when Mark and I worked together to parse the narrative structure in Harriet Doerr's incredible *Stones for Ibarra*, or I blanched openly in our discussion of Cormac McCarthy's truly gruesome *Blood Meridian* (seriously, *so* much scalping), I know now it was a kind of courtship. There's nothing that makes me say "I-want-to-have-your-children" more than a bearded, hazel-eyed man in snug Levi's analyzing George Eliot's limber and muscular handling of point of view in *Middlemarch*. My beating heart.

Near the end of that semester, I saw Mark at a happy hour; we were both still partnered, but both relationships were disintegrating, winding down. In possibly the worst pickup line in the deep history of MFA-program mating, I asked him if he'd be willing to give me an electronic copy of the handout he'd made outlining the fundamental elements in a great work of literature and aligning them with James Welch's *Fools Crow*. He was delighted to oblige, but neither of us can find the list now. In truth, I really *did* want that list.

The only element I remember is fire.

A short winter passes, and now it is spring in Tuscaloosa. Villainously, I have ended my own fizzled three-year romance and have been hooking up after hours with a fellow graduate student anxious to cloak our lascivious mischief under the cover of darkness. His secret is safe with me, but even as I'm going about complicating with late-night liaisons the plot of the real love story I am trying to tell, some news catches my ear: Mark's relationship is on the rocks. The scuttlebutt around the program is that he's moved out of the apartment he had shared with his librarian girlfriend, taking his shaggy mutt, Walt, with him. The magnolia is in full, fragrant bloom, and everything that happens next unfolds in the present tense with no time for reflection, which is the way with early love.

Another stranger is coming to town. Gerald Stern is coming to read, and I want to do something special for his reception, something impressive. I decide on cheese twists made from homemade puff pastry dough.

Have you ever made puff pastry dough from scratch? It takes *days*. That dough requires a lover, not a baker, but perhaps I'm drawing a distinction where there should be none. The détrempe is simple: flour, salt, butter, and icy cold water. I use my grandmother's pastry cutter with the smooth green handle to cut in the butter. Then the water, a little kneading with just the fingertips, and into the fridge to chill for eight hours. Puff pastry requires foresight. Think of her in the night. In the morning, roll her into a rectangle, gently, and then take a large hunk of butter and press it into a rectangular shape: a butter baby—the better the butter, the better the baby. Place the baby—gently, gently—in the center of the rolled détrempe, and fold over the doughy edges. Swaddle the baby. (Note that the dough and the butter should be of an equal consistency and temperature—this is harder than it might sound on a warm spring day in Alabama. Use care.) Roll the dough and her butter into a perfect rectangle. Fold in thirds, like a love letter. Rotate ninety degrees. Repeat. Chill. Repeatrepeatrepeat. On the third morning, cut and shape your cheese sticks. Use the finest Parmigiano-Reggiano, cheese no graduate student can afford. Bake. Cool. Arrange in a sloping wooden bowl. Gorgeous. Tuck them in with a tea towel to keep them safe.

At the party for Gerald Stern, watch this scene unfold as if you're watching an episode of *Seinfeld*. First, the guy you're currently carrying on with, but in the most clandestine and casual of ways, approaches the food table, drawn to your golden twists. He selects one from the basket, pulls it toward his gaping mouth, and takes a big bite. Then there's some sputtering, and he spits flaking pastry into the palm of his hand. This is what he says, with a pronounced Arkansas twang: "Da-amn! I thought that was gonna be a *breadstick!*"

You say nothing. What can you say? You're still standing there, aghast, when Mark—that guy from Keeble's class who can really wear a pair of jeans and made that smart literary-elements handout—fills the vacated space at the table. The other guy has gone off to find a trash can for the thrice-chewed head of one of your lovingly shaped twists. Mark has not witnessed the absurd display of his unknown rival. He too selects a golden spiral from the bowl and takes a bite. "Mmm." He smiles and takes another bite. And then, looking directly into your eyes, he says, "Wow. Someone made puff pastry. Did *you?*"

Yes, as a matter of fact, yes, yes I did.

The next scene serves as the climax in the core marriage story, and in fact, the featured sport parallels the graphic Professor Keeble smoothed onto the blackboard with white chalk during the sprung novel class: a big circle punctured by a sharp arrow. This is the picture of every story, he told us. The Insider encounters the Other, two worlds collide, someone goes on a journey, something versus anything else, and, yes, a stranger comes to town. When I think about Keeble's picture like a seventh-grade boy, it strikes me as a little dirty. Also, it's a dartboard, and in 1999, Tuesday nights in Tuscaloosa always began with half-price margaritas at Pepito's on the campus strip and ended downtown at The Chukker—where our game was darts.

On this decisive night, we're finishing up a round of Cricket, girls against boys. I'm wearing my favorite jeans—tight, faded Levi's with some lace around the ankles. I steady my wedge heels, line up my shot down the point of the only shining thing in that dark bar, and let the cool steel fly from my fingers—arrow into circle—closing out our sixteens and putting an extra twenty points on our male opponents. My female partner in crime, Anna, whoops, and I swagger from the beer-and-cigarette shelf on one side of the narrow room to the board on the other to pull the needle tips from the cork.

Bar games are all about asses, aren't they? Pool, foosball, darts. So many circles, so many arrows. There are eight guys behind me, including my future husband, and before I stretch up to give that dart at the top of the twenty a good, firm yank, I position my feet in their two-inch wedge heels just right, feeling the heat from the men's eyes warm my jeans like I'm sitting on a dryer. I twirl around fetchingly. "Britney Spears or Gwen Stefani?"

This is a game we've dubbed "the margarita game" for obvious reasons. I've thrown out an easy one, I know, although certainly revealing in terms of character. The object of the margarita game is to choose which celebrity you'd rather have sex with and defend that choice. Sometimes this requires serious deliberation and fine distinctions of desire and revulsion—Jennifer Aniston or Courteney Cox? Superman or Spiderman? Wayne Newton or Randy Newman? Olivia Newton John or Linda Ronstadt? Sting or Bono?—but this one is a no-brainer.

Anna grins a swimming grin through the smoke. She's on to me. I repeat my challenge. "Britney Spears or Gwen Stefani?"

The swarthy Arkansan I've been going home with on Tuesday nights, the one who spit out my cheese twist, doesn't hesitate. "Britney Spears."

Anna's left eyebrow arches up as high and bright as an exit sign.

The hazel-eyed Illinoisan I *want* to go home with, the one who praised my puff pastry, comes in right behind him. "Britney Spears? Are you *kidding*, man? Gwen Stefani. Totally."

Anna smiles. I grin back at her and then at Mark. Of course, nothing can ever be the same again.

In love, timing is everything. Last call came and went, and then we gathered our smoky leather jackets, cigarettes, and darts and headed out into the night. On the street, in the muted glow of the beer signs, Mark's eyes found mine. In the same moment, my newly outed Spears-loving friend figured it was just a regular Tuesday and went to stand by the passenger door of my car. Mark saw this and looked away.

"Good night," I said as meaningfully as I could muster, trying to get Mark to again meet my eyes. He would not.

What a disaster.

When we got to my friend's apartment, I turned off the car, didn't get out, and didn't waste time. "We can't do this anymore," I told him. "I think Mark and I are going to see what we might be able to get going." That's all I remember. I gave him a kiss on the cheek. "Good night."

Frankly, he seemed fine with it. "Okay," he said. "Good night." And he got out of my car.

I drove home, suffering over what Mark thought I was doing. I hated that right that moment he believed I had somehow failed to notice the current connecting our bodies that night, glowing red and hot like lava flow, like *fire*. He couldn't think he'd been making that up, right?

Shit shit shit.

I sat in the dark, silent car for long minutes, considering. It was two in the morning. People who aren't crazy don't call other people who aren't crazy for a first real date at two in the morning. "No, they don't," I said aloud to myself, pulling my reluctant keys from the ignition. I didn't need to wait long, but I did need to wait until morning. I made myself get into my own bed and stay there.

Poor thing. Bless her heart. I wish I could tell the shamed and sleepless girl I was that night to take a deep, cleansing breath, drink some water, get some rest, and get ready to enjoy the slide down the denouement. Love is an art. Love takes practice. Objectively, I think we can agree that she was making some pretty good, principled, forward-looking choices for a young woman with two beaus in the wee hours of a steamy, tequila-fueled Alabama night.

Nine in the morning seemed like the right time to call. Banker's hours. Rising as we were from the smoky, beery mire of margarita night, the pursuit of fresh possibility and a lifetime of passion, joy, and commitment was no doubt a lot to ask. "Can I come over?" I asked. "I want to talk to you."

Mark sounded wary. "Okay," he said. "Come on over."

He lived in a crappy apartment in a crappy part of town. As I climbed the water-stained, stinking stairs, my heart sped ahead of me. Did I know I was climbing the stairs to the rest of my life? I think I did. I really do. Mark opened the door and led me out onto a worn, gray deck jutting out over the overgrown, postage-stamp yard. The concrete walls were lost in a tangle of kudzu, and the insect drone buzzed like a live wire. "I'm sorry," I said. "I didn't know what to do." Then I told him why I was there at 9:00 a.m. on a Wednesday like some sort of crazy person—but not as crazy as a 2:00 a.m. crazy person—but of course, he already knew. And he forgave me for the night before. He understood. Marriage is an arrangement of perpetual forgiveness.

At about 4:00 p.m. that first day, as we sat on the dingy gray carpet (there was no couch yet) nearing the end of the world's worst first-date movie, *American History X*, Mark leaned closer and closer, occluding Ed Norton and his swastika tattoo, and said, finally, "I think I'm going to have to kiss you now."

I didn't leave for three days.

A few weeks later, we'll be lying together on his twin mattress like naked spoons under a sheet, and Mark will say in my ear: *Would you like me to say a poem for you?*

Yes.

Since feeling is first, he will begin, stroking my naked hip with his warm fingers—my skin, his skin, the soft sheet—and I will think . . . no, I won't think. I'll just be. I just am. I will be there in Mark's bed, our giant dogs on their respective beds, also loving each other from their first day, and I will be wholly happy. I don't think: this is too soon, this will not last, this cannot be real. I just listen to Mark saying the poem, Cummings, my body an instrument to this happiness, filled. In the warm curve of my neck, the tiniest hairs there blown by the breath of his words, he finishes:

> lady i swear by all flowers. Don't cry
> —the best gesture of my brain is less than
> your eyelids' flutter which says
>
> we are for each other: then
> laugh, leaning back in my arms
> for life's not a paragraph
>
> And death i think is no parenthesis

That was sixteen years ago. There were many close calls. Mistakes were made but also dreams and plans. A shotgun wedding with the most beautiful flowers. And now? We are thriving. Five nights out of seven we gather around our dining room table, light candles, choose music, pour wine or chocolate soy milk, depending, and love each other, all of us.

The kids know our family began way down south in Alabama when Mom and Dad were in school, the narrative stacking up, folding over like butter in well-tended dough, gaining richness. They know about Grammy Sarah and her wild parties. They know about Uncle Ian's burning, and how Mom was born too late. They know all about the giant crocodile named Cookie and the poor chickens. Recently, when I told our daughter a PG version of the puff pastry story, she seemed satisfied that her dad had been the sophisticated one, the one with good taste, the one who had pleased me—the other man, the one who could have undone her, rejecting and rejected.

How close we come at every corner, in every generation, to having different stories to tell to an entirely different audience of beloveds. In any lasting love story, seriously, what are the *chances*?

In the dancing light of our table's candles, I watch our children's sweet faces, both with Mark's nose, mouth, and chin but, like a superhero mask, my blue eyes. Through the speakers, Gillian Welch sings *That's the way the cornbread crumbles, that's the way the whole thing ends*, and I remember the unlikely setting of our family's beginning, a bar so dive they tore it down, but not before that dart game, not before the arrow penetrated the circle, not before Mark could give the right answer in the back room of The Chukker where the smoke was the thickest.

There, halfway between the dartboards and the beer-and-cigarette shelf, in a tunnel of moving air blown through the haze by a single, humming box fan, in the cradle of my too-tight jeans, the ovum who would be our first, our baby girl, shielded her stinging eyes from the smoke and perked up her ears to hear her daddy's voice: "Gwen Stefani. Totally."

And the poet prince and the more narratively inclined princess lived ever after, braiding legs and language and deoxyribonucleic acid.

Happily.

PART II

we are for each other

FAMILY PORTRAIT

She was in the grocery store sulking past forbidden sugar cereals when she stopped, looked around, and realized she could put a box of Froot Loops in her cart if she wanted. Could she? She was thirty-four years old. She did. Nobody stopped her—who would stop her?—but she kept checking her back until she made it out to the parking lot and got all the bags into the car.

At home, the milk turned a putrid gray, and even dry, the bright sugar rings weren't as good as she remembered them. She sat at the wooden table in the kitchen with the baby, sliding the red ones into place for the top arc of a cereal rainbow and remembering the Atari her brother had won back in the midseventies with his drawing of Toucan Sam in the Kellogg's "Stick up for Breakfast" contest. The only game was Pong, a drifting dot and two straight-line paddles locked in a perpetual bling-boing-bling. How would she ever communicate to her new-millennium daughter the excitement, the *thrill*, of the day that Atari arrived in its plain brown box? For months, her brother—celebrated artist, creator of the winning Sam-in-the-jungle scene—reigned as king of the neighborhood.

She was down to the greens in her ROY G. BIV rainbow when she realized something, something big: they could catch a plane. Her little family of three could fly out of dreary, frozen Indiana and celebrate the rest of Christmas vacation somewhere sunny—and alone. This was revelatory. A full year into her daughter's life and Jill suddenly understood that *she* was the mother.

She chose a family-run hotel in Madeira Beach near St. Petersburg. Their room had a little kitchen with one of those undersized stoves and a too-bright fluorescent light, but the double glass doors looked out over the bay where the proprietor seemed always to be busy on his sailboat, *Island Woman*. That's the thing about men and their boats, she thought—they can never get enough. There's always something to fiddle with, a reason to pull her out of the water, sink her back in, sand her down, shine her up. A man with a boat never lacks for something to do.

Her own husband, boatless, was still sleeping in the king-sized bed under the giant straw fan, and Jill sat cross-legged next to the baby tossing Cheerios onto the tray of her booster chair. They faced the water and the man. Boat TV. A pelican—the baby's first!—sailed in and landed hard on a piling. "Look, Ella! Look! A pelican!" She could have called that bird anything—a seagull, a loon, an osprey, or an ostrich for heaven's sake—and the baby would have believed her.

That afternoon, they set up the booster chair on a picnic table and drank margaritas and ate blackened grouper sandwiches on the dock. The baby munched fries and smeared ketchup in her hair. Men in tight suits buzzed by in weird parachute machines that reminded Jill of the jet-pack police in *Fahrenheit 451*. A gull dove down to steal a fry, and her husband covered his head with his hands, threatened to scream like a little girl.

That night was New Year's Eve, and she fell asleep on the couch in front of the glass doors despite the blasts of color exploding over the water. Her husband woke her up with a midnight kiss just as Regis talked the ball down in Times Square (Regis? Where's Dick Clark?), and they went together into the bedroom to kiss their sleeping angel on her fat cheeks. She felt a kind of surreal happiness and thought: This is probably as good as it gets.

The next afternoon, while the other two napped, Jill took her book down to the dock to show her Indiana-white legs to the Florida sun and breathe in some air the wind had cleaned on the salty water. She found a spot on a bench, and another sea plane pelican, all pouch and hold, skimmed low across the water, eyes trained down, looking to scoop up some morsels, swallow them whole and squirming. From a distance, the pelican had seemed so exotic. Up close, she could see the pelican was filthy, mangy. A dirty bird.

She was never alone for long these days. Her book wasn't even cracked before a little girl came skipping down the planks of the dock on her bare feet and cast a towel in a flap of rainbow colors down on the warm wood. "Mmm," the girl said. "I think I'll set up *here* for a while!"

She was six, she reported, her name was Cameron, and she was here in Florida with her mom and dad for a whole *week*. After this they'd go to see her sister's *baby*, who had just learned to walk. Cameron wanted to know if Jill had any sisters or babies, and she told the girl, feeling lucky, that she had both. "Two sisters and one baby, my own little girl, also one, who's sleeping up in the room." Cameron took that in, then mentioned the brother she never saw. He was in some kind of trouble, but she's wasn't sure. She'd like to see all of them more—the sister with the baby, the baby, the brother—but she was careful to let Jill know they didn't all live together. They couldn't. They lived all over the country. *All* over the country. Jill noticed Cameron's flare for emphasis, one word in every sentence, often where she'd least expect it.

As Cameron talked, lying on her belly, her bare feet stirred the air in rapid circles and her palms patted the colors of her towel. Every paragraph or two, she required a bit of information. "Do you have any *brothers*?"

"Yes," Jill reported, "and he has a little girl exactly your age." Jill's eyes flicked up to the mother lying by the kidney-shaped pool, a pool only big enough for children to really get going in but beautiful in a tropical way, palm trees and shine. She looked to be about forty, so she would have been about Jill's age when she had Cameron. Not a young mother. The other woman's sunglasses pointed down toward her book. An older man sat two lounge chairs away, talking business on a cell phone—probably almost sixty, and that explained the sister with the baby, the brother too far away to see, maybe in some kind of trouble . . .

Cameron popped up from her towel, all long brown legs and round eyes. She couldn't stay down for long. She was made of springs and tendons. "Well," she said, "I guess I'd better *throw* these shells back in the water so they can become sand!" She produced a handful of shells out of nowhere and scuttled to the edge of the dock, still chattering about the fish she saw earlier, bigger than these little fish, *much* bigger, but *look* at all those fish now. Do you *see* them? And she cast the tiny white shells, like beads or confetti, across the calm surface of the water; they sprayed down, a lovely sprinkle of sound. Together they watched them sink through interested fish and onto the sandy bottom. "Watch," Cameron instructed, "now watch." The sand on the bottom shifted and danced—was it moving all that time?—and Cameron's luminescent shells absorbed into the tawny grains. "See? See? Now they will become sand."

Although she'd be loath to confess, Jill wasn't always one to enjoy the company of other people's children, but she liked this Cameron. She sparkled, but the way she talked to her was terrifying. Jill found herself wishing she wouldn't tell her so much. There were too many things not to trust in this world, and a strange lady sitting on a dock was probably one of them. Also, there was something behind Cameron's eyes, something old. Something that reminded her of herself.

Her husband walked down to the dock carrying the baby. Ella squinted into the bright light to marvel at the lively creature standing next to her mother, so much better than a pelican. "This is *my* baby," Jill told Cameron. "This is Ella." Cameron reached out for Ella's cheeks and pinched them just as an old woman might do. Ella hated to be pinched, but she didn't cry. Cameron's eyes were too round. Too much like her own eyes.

With a bigger audience, Cameron turned business-like, played the experienced tourist. After all, she had been there for a *week*. She gave her review of the Dalí museum. At first, they heard "dolly" because she was six, but that misimpression didn't last long. "You have to touch the fur when you first go in. It's red. You have to touch it." Cameron was full of instructions. "Then you look into this box and it's like a frame. Inside it's a face, but it's not a face. There are two pictures on the wall and they're the eyes. Then there's a fire. That's the nose. And a couch is the mouth."

For the rest of the afternoon, Cameron trailed Jill and the baby wherever they went on the hotel grounds. She followed them when they took the bag with the dirty diapers to the dumpster, and then she skipped behind them until her nose pressed against the glass door of their room. She must have known she wasn't supposed to come in, that she hadn't been invited, but she came terribly close. "We're in four," Cameron announced. "Right there." Pointing. "Okay, I guess. I'll see you later." When she backed away, her eyes were funny, darting around to see if anybody was watching.

Shouldn't somebody be watching?

Jill remembered a time when she was a graduate teaching assistant at the University of Alabama, hanging out with boys, the kind of boys a good feminist wouldn't hang out with on a normal day—body-ogling, PBR-swigging boys who were fun to play pool with because they were smart and funny and could quote poetry even when they were many, many sheets to the wind. These boys were graduate teaching assistants just like her.

One day, an out-of-a-magazine co-ed from her English 101 class came into her office weeping about her life, pledging that she would do *anything* to make a C in the class. She was wearing a tank top over another tank top, both Lycra, no bra, and she put her breasts on the desk. Put them there. The act seemed unconscious—why would it be otherwise?—but there they were, placed there, like a bottle of Coke or a literature anthology. On the desk. And Jill couldn't help but look at them, sitting there. She explained about the final paper and the revision process, but she was thinking: *Shit. My God. What if I wasn't me? What if I was one of those boys?*

Later, entering the red mouth of the Dalí museum in St. Petersburg, Jill stopped to peer into the hole, and with one hand on the baby's stroller and the other on Dalí's box, she could see that Cameron remembered everything exactly: the frame eyes, the fire nose, the couch mouth. "Don't you think that's pretty impressive, Mark?" she asked her husband. "She's only six."

"Not really," her husband said. "That's what you remember. You remember what's at the beginning and what's at the end."

She put her own eyes back up to the box and forced her mind to turn: a face, a living room, a face, a living room. The baby tossed her Dalí finger puppet onto the floor, and Jill took this as a signal to keep moving.

When they pulled into the hotel parking lot, she waved when she saw Cameron in the back seat of a white rental car. Cameron looked down without waving back. Jill couldn't see the other mother's eyes beneath her dark sunglasses, but she could tell she was looking right at her. The other mother's mouth was a straight line, a couch—no cushions. More of a bench, really.

In the morning, Cameron was not by the pool. The family had checked out.

Jill was disappointed. She had wanted to thank Cameron for recommending the museum. She wanted to tell her they'd touched the red fur, and everything in the box was just as Cameron had said it would be. She'd remembered exactly: a face, a living room, a face . . . and still, she had imagined saying to Cameron, *There's no place to relax, is there? No place to sit, not without messing up the face. What's that blot on the mouth? A bad tooth? A canker? Oh. No.*

It's Dad, sitting on the couch. Jill had thought maybe this would make Cameron laugh. Such a serious little girl—she had wanted to make her laugh.

Outside the glass doors, the man worked on his boat, sanding down the bowsprit. He whistled while he worked. The day was so perfect, the sun on the water, it made her eyes hurt. Under the rippling surface, Jill imagined Cameron's shells, everything becoming sand.

She wiped the applesauce from the baby's face with a wet cloth and walked to the open door of the bedroom. She could see her husband lying spread-eagle on the floral bedspread. The straw fan on the wall was a kind of sombrero, the open fingers on each of his hands a fringe of flirty lashes, eyeball palms, head and torso nose, legs forming those lines that trace from our noses to the edges of our lips—what were those lines *called*?—but no mouth. She imagined curling herself onto the bottom of the bed to finish the picture. She could reach up and around her husband's feet, touch her fingers and toes to bold hibiscus cheeks on the horrible bedspread, and become a grinning mouth. Maybe she could grab the baby from her chair and plunk her, round and perfect, on the bottom corner. She could be a mole. A beauty mark!

Yes, she thought, scooping up the baby. That's what you remember. You remember what's at the beginning and what's at the end. Even if nobody was there to see her, she would be the smile.

THE ELEVEN-MINUTE CRIB NAP

Babies don't cut deals, and right now my tapping keyboard sounds like the clicking heels of an efficient secretary leading the negotiators into the boardroom. The last thing I want to do is engage. I'd take my laptop into another room, farther away from the crib, but there are too many risks: the scraping of my chair, that squeaky board at the edge of the dining room, the real possibility that a tangle of cords could crash the mouse to the floor. Better I stay put.

I just spent the first hour of what should have been a two-hour nap for Ella nursing her to sleep. She slept, yes, forehead damp with the pleasure of milk and Mama, both of us smelling of honey and salt, her bare toes leveraging my open palm, flexing and pushing. I can't blame her for wanting to stay in my arms, but I'm a teacher with a pile of grading and a roomful of anxious twenty-year-olds waiting for me in the morning. Everybody wants a piece of me. So with my finger at the corner of Ella's lip, I broke the seal between our bodies. There was a tiny pop as I coaxed my nipple from her mouth. I held a gentle pressure on her chin while her jaw's pumping wound down. Good.

But when I rose from the chair, walked the three steps to the crib with all the stealth of a cat burglar, and started to tip Ella's meticulously supported head toward the mattress, her lids popped open like those of the long-lashed baby dolls of my childhood with their disturbingly glossy marble-blue eyes. Except in reverse. The eye-popping happens when I lay Ella down, not when I tilt her up. Tip. Pop. Hair-curling scream.

I tried to explain to my nearly toddling daughter that she had this all wrong. I tried to make her understand that our arrangement was only fair. "After all," I said, wincing and patting her belly in what I intended to be the soothing strokes of all the baby-care books, "I already held you for half the nap! Most babies your age don't have that kind of luck, you know. Some babies go to group care where somebody else takes care of them all day while their mommies work. Can you imagine? But not you. No, sweetie pie. Not you. You get to have half your nap with Mommy, and then you get to have the second half in your crib so Mommy can grade some essays. Mommy needs her hands to grade essays."

My tone was distinctly Faye Dunaway in *Mommy Dearest*, and the patting was provoking: too fast, too desperate—not at all pacifying. In that first run at the crib, I'd succeeded not only in waking Ella but riling her into an uncommon rage. She thrashed, face twisted in fury like the Heat Miser in the holiday cartoon, sweaty hair poking everywhere, her own personal crown of thorns. Ella didn't want to reason with me, and she didn't want to talk compromise.

I scooped her up to begin again. Back to the rocker we went. If suckling at a mother's breast can be disgruntled, that's how Ella nursed now, her one exposed eye wide open and glaring. She wanted me to know she had my number. Rock, rock, rock.

I hummed the sleepy song, her so-called trigger song. According to the books, this soft melody, sung over and over, with the pleasure and consistency of repetition (oh, the repetition of new motherhood!), would let our baby know that the time had come to sleep. *I went down in the river to pray* . . . Our song comes off the *O Brother, Where Art Thou?* soundtrack. Remember that hypnotic scene with all the slow-moving, white-clad church members walking into the muddy river to be washed free of sin and transgression? Delmar splashes through the water and up to the preacher for his dunking. What better soundtrack for nap time? Baptism and sleep aren't so different. Each provides a fresh beginning.

Ella and I were stuck in a movie of our own making, and of course, because I had to sing without pause or ceasing, eventually I departed from the words I learned from Alison Krauss and made up my own: *Oh, Eeeeelllla, let's go down, let's go down, come on down . . .* Then the daddies went down and the mommies. Eventually, the grandmas and the uncles and the puppies made their way down to that baptismal river. Everybody except Ella, it seemed, went on down.

Instead of signaling sleep, all my singing and rocking had marked my agenda, my trickery. I will not sleep, Ella's one eye said. I will not, I will not, I will not. Rock and sing. *Oh, brother, let's go down, let's go down, come on down, oh, brother . . .* Oh brother, indeed. Fifteen minutes later, she seemed out once again. I untangled her fingers from the fabric of my t-shirt, lifted her arm a few inches, and dropped her hand. The arm dropped like a soggy teething toy into a basket. Thunk. Sleeping.

I considered my options. I could stay in the chair with Ella on my lap. I had the stack of essays within reach, and if I could prop up her head with rolled blankets (also within reach) and extract my right arm from under her head, I could stabilize an essay on a hardcover copy of *Horton Hears a Who* and get some grading done. I did this for twenty minutes, making it through an essay and a half. Then I had to pee. *Besides,* I thought, *this is absurd. Who does this? I am a mockery to working mothers everywhere. I am a slave to my baby.*

Again, I stood over the crib with a slumbering Ella.

I had a different strategy in mind. This time, I would leave my nipple in her mouth as we descended together into the crib. Apparently, her mattress had been rigged with a touch-activated shocking device because as soon as her back touched the sheet: Bam. Thrash. Scream. I chased her shrieking face with my breast, pointing my nipple at her vibrating uvula, like a target-shooting game at the state fair. But I didn't have a chance to aim. Ella thrashed from side to side. She was a crazy person on a cop show being subdued, an alligator and I was the wrestler, an epileptic and I had the wooden spoon.

Then, finally, in a moment that was lucky or inevitable, I caught her lower lip with the nipple in just the right way and instinct kicked in. She latched on, and her cries muffled. She sucked. The sobs became hiccups. Her eyes closed, but her jaw kept working. Insofar as such a thing is possible when you are a woman bent at the waist, forehead resting on a pee pad, both breasts dangling, I relaxed. *I might as well*, I thought. I knew I would have to stay like that for at least ten more minutes, or until I could again lift her hand, release, and watch it fall back to the sheet. That gave me ten good minutes to evaluate my situation.

Am I a good mother or a bad mother? I wondered. Certainly, I am wrapped around my baby's Napoleonic finger. But aren't I loving and attentive when I'm unwilling to abandon a baby, an innocent baby, who obviously feels insecure without me? Then again, is it my *fault* that she feels insecure without me?

Torn between Dr. Bill Sears's affirmations of attachment parenting and the guilt I felt for not even really trying the popular sleep-training methods espoused by Dr. Richard Ferber, I realized, with a start, that the advising voices in my head both belonged to *dudes*, neither of whom were in this room with their heads smashed against a pee pad.

Soundlessly muttering curses at Sears and Ferber, I lifted Ella's curled fingers a couple inches off the mattress and let go. The hand dropped. This time, the small, falling fist looked to me like the Times Square ball, super slow-mo, easing down the wire with seconds ticking down. Clunk. Party time.

I slipped my nipple out and held it there on her lower lip for another count of ten. Standing, mother erectus, a final trial stood between me and freedom—or, at least, me and the rest of those essays. I needed to fold the top bar up on the crib and lock it into position. Again, the sadistic elves in the crib-making factory had played me for a sucker. Do you know the sound the door of a haunted mansion makes in a horror movie when the stupid kids push on it to make their way into the dark hall hanging with cobwebs? Then you also know the moaning screech of this bar rising up into position. Are you familiar with the sound a pogo stick makes when an exuberant child slams the pavement, jamming the spring into a tight coil and then boinging upward with a great, metallic release? Yes. This was the sound the hinges on either side of the crib bar made when I pulled them with my sweating fingers and gently eased them into a locked position. There was a one in three chance Ella would sleep through this noise. But despite the inauspicious beginning, this was turning into my lucky day. Ella kept sleeping.

And do you know what I do? I do not grade the essays. In an act of restless, artistic selfishness, I write the above. I write about loud cribs and soft nipples and the places I am willing to rest my head. Just as I am about to further indulge in a moment of existential angst about the fragmented, interrupted writing that is born of motherhood, even before the good feminist in me kicks in to defend the domestic and all that it contains, I hear a wavering cry.

Ella is awake. I see her from my chair, and she does not look rested. Oh, brother.

THE GOOGLY EYE

Mark had gone to work, and Ella and I were sitting at the kitchen table eating avocado sandwiches. Ella was not quite three.

Laying a finger aside of her nose, Santa-style, Ella looked me in the eye and said, "Mommy. My nose hurts." She paused. "I have a googly eye in my nose."

A "googly eye," in our family lexicon, is a three-dimensional white eyeball containing a shiny black disc that jiggles around behind a transparent plastic cornea. That's what makes it googly. (I Googled "googly eyes" and learned they're also called "wiggle eyes" or "moveable paste-on eyes.") Googly eyes are flat on one side—the paper side, the side used for gluing eyeballs of various sizes to paper, shells, and upside-down egg cartons to make monsters, crabs, and silly caterpillars. The other side, the googly side, is convex, like the surface of a real eyeball. The googly eyes Ella's babysitter had brought over to stick onto funny monkey faces a few days earlier were big ones, at least half an inch across—not the kind of thing you'd want to have in your nose, especially if you were three and in possession of such a *small* nose.

I considered all this as I chewed a suddenly over-large mouthful of bread that had turned hard and dry between my teeth. Washing it down with a gulp of lemonade, I studied Ella's face, her miniature button nose. *How would a half-inch googly eye fit in that itsy bitsy nose?* Pulse quickening, I mustered all my parenting skills to keep my voice level and calm. As with most circumstances involving human error, I began with denial. "What, honey? What did you say?"

She was watching me as carefully as I was watching her. Ella knew I had heard *exactly* what she'd said.

"Oh, Mommy," she said, reading the panic under my act. She tossed her hair back in mock hilarity. "No! I don't have a googly eye in my nose! Ha ha *ha*! I don't. I was just kidding you around, Mommy."

I didn't know what to do. How did she even think to say a thing like that? *I have a googly eye in my nose.*

"Honey," I said. "Do you have a googly eye in your nose?"

"No," she said, glaring now. "I said I was *kidding* you around!"

I let it rest. Maybe together we could pretend this one out of existence. And really, how could Ella have a googly eye up her nose? That would be nuts. That would be a medical emergency. And furthermore, how would it have gotten there? Ella's a smart girl. She wouldn't be foolish enough to insert a googly eye into her nostril. Who would do such a thing? Why?

An hour later, I tiptoed into her room to check on her during her nap. She was snoring like a piglet. I put my face right up to her face as she lay on her pillow, cheeks pink, blond hair sticking every which way, cherubic as all get up. The snore really was more squeal than snore, and—was I imagining this?—the sound seemed to be coming from just one nostril. The right nostril. Yes. A kind of whistling wheeze.

While Ella slept, I consulted a book. Foreign objects, Nostril. The book said to not, under any circumstances, attempt to remove the object at home using a pair of tweezers. *Tweezers!* I thought. *Of course! What a good idea!* I read on. The removal process was a delicate one, and not only could a hapless, panicky parent with a pair of tweezers damage the delicate nasal tissue, she could also make matters worse by a) lodging the object more deeply in the nose, or b) actually pushing the object into the throat, which could cause choking. The thing to do, the book said, was to call the doctor.

I considered a plan of action, contemplating the possibility that this was all in my mind, and waited for Ella to wake up. I leaned over her face and studied her nose. Was that a lump on the right side?

Meanwhile, Mark was still at work. Talking about poetry.

When Ella woke up, I was waiting. She sat up and rubbed her nose. She whimpered and repeated her confession: "My nose hurts."

I pulled a book light from a shelf and sat on the edge of her bed. "Okay, honey. I'm just going to look up your nose and see what I see."

As I moved in with the light, I heard echoes of that fierce child from William Carlos Williams's "The Use of Force"—the flushed and feverish girl the country doctor has to hold down, using a big silver spoon to pry open her teeth so he can see her throat. It wasn't quite that bad, but Ella fought. Just as the wild-haired, blue-eyed Mathilda refuses to reveal, and thus confirm, her diagnosis—diphtheria—Ella wanted to hide her own disaster. "No, Mommy! I was kidding you around! I don't have a googly eye in my nose! I don't, I don't . . ."

Swinging a leg over her little body, I pinned her forehead to the pillow with my left hand. Gently. Then I angled the thin beam of the book light up into her right nostril.

How do I describe what it was to look up into my preschooler's nose and see an eye, a *googly* eye, staring back at me? Accumulating mucus had slicked the surface, giving the eye a shining, evil glint. Ella twisted under my hold and let out a squeaky cry. In this sudden burst of air, the eye shifted and the dark pupil rattled with a menacing shimmy. I wanted to scream. Holy shit. But good, calm, handling-things mothers don't scream when they shine lights into their children's noses, do they? Even if there's someone there, staring them down? I blinked and looked again. Crap.

I flicked off the light and released my grip on Ella's forehead.

"Okay," I said. "Okay. Okay, sweetie, there *is* a googly eye in your nose."

I wanted to grab the tweezers and get the eyeball the hell out of Ella's nose. Of course I did. But I restrained myself and walked steadily to the phone. I am no good in a crisis. I have friends and relations, quite a few actually, who work as nurses and doctors in emergency rooms. This is what they *choose to do*. Not me. I simply don't possess the disposition. But Mark was gone, talking about poetry with a gaggle of adoring undergrads, and I was home with our daughter. Our daughter and the shuddering creature lodged in her small nostril.

I dialed Ella's pediatrician. It was four o'clock. Of course it was. The nurse explained that because it was so late in the afternoon, there was no time to squeeze Ella in, but she reminded me that the after-hours emergency pediatric clinic, Prime-Time, would be opening in an hour. If we got there early to check in, we might be able to avoid a long wait. "Don't try to get it out yourself," she said before I hung up. "Really. Don't."

I was so tempted. This whole ordeal could be over in thirty seconds. By the time Mark got home, it could be a funny story instead of a medical emergency. We would eat dinner. I would finish grading that stack of essays.

Lining up all the tweezers I had in the bathroom, I chose a pair with a satisfyingly tapered and blunted tip. What could it hurt? I turned them over in my fingertips. Glint. How tempted we humans are to follow one misstep with another. *I could fix this*, I thought. *Yes, mistakes were made, but if I do this right, I could get us all out of this mess. In an instant, everything could be okay.*

Tweezers in hand, I checked my watch and called Mark, who was just then getting out of class.

"She has a *what* in her nose?"

"A googly eye," I repeated, and then I broached the plan with the blunt-tipped tweezers.

"No," Mark said. "Jill. No."

Now, at least, I had someone to be mad at for this mess. Now, thanks to Mark, the risk was too great, and I would *not* be able to make it all better. Plus, where had he been in our hour of need?

"Fine," I snapped. "Just come home then. We'll be ready to go by the time you get here."

With Ella, I remained upbeat. "Sweetheart! Come to Mommy so I can give you a nice *hairdo!*" My inflection was cloying, way off. Ella eyed me suspiciously, and I imagined her third eye, rattling, sharing her disapproval. My own mother calls me "sweetheart" when she is feeling one of two emotions: annoyance or helplessness. Here, the false-ringing endearment contained nuances of both.

At Prime-Time Pediatrics, I answered all the receptionist's questions with a straight face.

"Reason for visit?"

"She has a googly eye in her nose."

"What?"

"You know, a googly eye. Those little plastic eyes you can glue on to make faces? A googly eye. I don't know how long it's been in there. And it's pretty big."

I wrote it that way on the form she slid across the counter to me: *googly eye in nose.* Later, on the bill, I noticed my description had been modified: *foreign object/nasal cavity.* Whatever.

The doctor's name was difficult to pronounce, but the nurse recognized this and told Ella she could call him "Dr. Rock." Dr. Rock was not a man of great humor, and so I tried to sit back and let him do his work without too much intervention on my part, but his gravitas made me edgy. He shone his special light up into Ella's nose. I can only imagine he saw the same thing I had. He flinched a tiny bit, mumbled something about taking a minute, and left the room. Dr. Rock didn't come back. Long minutes ticked by.

"He's looking it up," I whispered to Mark. "He doesn't know what to do."

We read the same *Sesame Street* board book over and over, and Dr. Rock remained gone.

When he finally returned, two nurses flanked him. *Shit*, I thought. *It's going to take three of them? What are they going to do to her? What does he think is going to happen here? Can't he just pull it out with a pair of tweezers?*

Indeed, he had a pair of tweezers, albeit super-long ones with an astounding slanting beak. The nurses were giggling a bit. One of them asked Ella why she did it. "Did you think you were going to be able to see up your own nose?"

Titter.

Ella didn't answer. She wasn't talking. Sensing the fear in the room, she sat in my lap as rigid as a stone.

The actual extraction was scary. First, Dr. Rock gave Ella a tissue and tried to get her to blow out the googly eye, but in my limited observation, nose-blowing is a skill that develops wondrously late in children. Even at almost three, Ella always sucked in instead of blowing out. Besides, she wasn't exactly in the mood to follow instructions.

Dr. Rock glided in on his wheeled stool.

They let me hold her. They never made me hand her over to the grinning nurses. That would have really freaked her out. It took way longer than I thought it should. It was not over in an instant. Dr. Rock was *verrrrry* deliberate and careful with his long tweezers, and there were many missed attempts. He had to wriggle the beak over the top of the googly eye and pull it down. This was a delicate operation.

Finally, out it came. The googly eye.

"Ugh," I said, "it's even bigger than I remembered it."

Dr. Rock held the googly eye aloft in his needle beak, both for the benefit of the nurses and his own consideration. He looked at Ella. "So now you know that we *never* put anything in our noses or our ears." I waited for the "smaller than your elbow" bit, but it never came. He plunked the googly eye onto a tissue and handed it to me. Ella, still snuffling, asked if she could take it home for her memory box. I agreed that was a good idea, and with the anxiety of our own situation abated, I quizzed Dr. Rock about the kinds of things he pulled out of kids' noses. I thought he was going to tell me that he extracted something from a nose every week or so, but in fact, he said the things-in-noses visits averaged three or four a year.

"I would have thought it would be more," I said. "What kinds of things do kids put in their noses?"

"Mostly vegetables," he said. "Beans, peas, things like that. Also, little stones." He finished writing on the billing report and handed it to me.

"What's the weirdest thing you've ever pulled out of someone's nose?"

Dr. Rock thought for a moment and then said, "A high-heeled shoe."

I gasped. "A *shoe*?!"

"Belonging to a Barbie," he clarified, raising his substantial eyebrows. Still, he didn't smile. *Silly, hysterical mother who doesn't supervise her kid well enough to prevent the introduction of foreign objects to the nasal cavity.* Then he shook our hands and left the room.

For her trouble, Ella got a purple Care Bear sticker, which she stuck in the bag with the sticky eye—the googliness of which seemed intensified, or maybe somehow *animated* from the time it had spent in a living body. Eek.

The next morning at breakfast, I asked Ella why she did it. What, I wanted to know, *compelled* her to stick that googly eye in her nose?

"I thought it would be different," she said, looking sad.

Oh, I thought. *Yes! That's it.* Ella's assessment explained a lifetime of my own biggest mistakes. *I thought it would be different.*

As a kid, when I jumped off the roof of the house with a garbage bag as a parachute, I thought it would be different. In high school, when I signed up for that course in trigonometry, I thought it would be different. Still in high school, when I climbed into the

Jeep with the way-too-old-for-me boy who'd been drinking Blue Hawaiians out of a milk jug, I thought it would be different. Having survived and made it to college, when I stuck out my tongue and accepted the proffered tab of LSD at the Oregon Country Fair, I thought it would be different. Later, in graduate school, and certainly old enough to know better, when I traipsed after my girlfriend in the steaming, snake-infested Alabama woods at midnight to find a skinny-dipping hole, I thought it would be different. When I was laboring with Ella and I refused to let the nurse find a vein and put in a hep-lock, *I thought it would be different.*

In all of these unfortunate circumstances, before I stepped forward and entered my own mistake, going too deep to extract myself without feeling the pain or embarrassment or both of my own bad choice, I thought it would be different. I neglected to consider how hard the ground, how unfathomable the function, how drunk the driver, how potent and troubling the drug, how thick the underbrush, and how much a woman can bleed. What, then, had I wanted? How had I thought it would be different? Well. I thought the bag might catch the air and carry me, like a paratrooper or a butterfly, gently to the ground; I thought my mastery of sines, cosines, and tangents—*Some Old Hippie Caught Another Hippie Tripping On Acid*—might elevate me to another level of intellectual superiority in my high school; I thought the boy in the Jeep might think me adventurous and cool and, in return, would love me; I thought the LSD might take me somewhere beautiful, away from the stinking porta potties and patchouli of the dusty fair to a place of pure happiness; I thought the swimming hole would be right down the road, just five minutes, and that the Alabama moon shining on the water would illuminate everything; and I thought I would give my baby safe and natural passage into this world without drugs or intervention.

I thought it would be different. Of course. I wondered what Ella had wanted when she stuck that eye up into her nostril. What had her desired outcome, that different ending, looked like to her?

"Different how?" I asked, watching her skewer a piece of waffle with a toothpick.

She couldn't say. "I thought it would be *different*," she repeated, as if that were all I needed to know, all I deserved to know. Maybe she thought the big googly eye wouldn't slide so easily into her nostril, but rather it would dangle humorously from the end of her nose and make everybody laugh. Maybe she thought she could stick things all over her face, as she and her babysitter had done to the monkey faces, and in this way become a kind of living craft project. Or maybe the giggling nurses were on to something. Maybe she thought if she stuck an eye up her nose she would be able to see the inside of her body.

Whatever the answer, Ella either didn't know why she'd pushed that googly eye into her nostril or she wasn't telling, but what struck me as I watched her crunch down her apple slices was how clearly she'd seemed to understand how we humans respond when we mess up. Not even three, and Ella had known she shouldn't tell. Her mistake would be her secret. How did she know that? Had we already modeled concealment for her? I gripped my coffee cup like a talisman, holding onto the lesson of the googly eye. I knew if I let that instinct for secrecy stick in my daughter and deepen, the next big error would be mine to regret.

"Can I play now?" Ella asked. I nodded, and she slid down from her booster seat, dutifully parroting Dr. Rock's good advice: "We *never* put anything in our ears or noses."

Right.

But then, what if we could stick googly eyes in our noses to see the dark secrets of our bodies? How cool would that be?

A STONE PEAR

On every visit, my great-aunt Mollie warned me that the fruit in the bowl on her dining room table was not real. Table and bowl both were carved from a deep, dark wood, and I remember still how irresistibly smooth the table felt beneath my fingers. This wood glowed, which I now know must have been the result of housekeepers wielding soft rags, but as a child I marveled at how these made objects showed off their glistening curves and joints, telling the story of their journey from the shaded forest to this well-lighted stretch of dining room in New Milford, Connecticut, and seeming—somehow—more real than real. So real, they were magic. I couldn't stop touching them.

The long, rectangular table stretches in my child's memory to seat at least twelve, and placed at the center, the focal point of the room, was that beautiful bowl, and in that bowl, the exquisitely fashioned fruit: two kinds of grapes, green and purple, two tawny pears, a handful of nectarines, and a single red apple. The fruit is fake, my aunt would remind me, not for eating. If I was hungry there were oranges in the icebox, or we could go down to the garden, duck under the bird nets, and pick some blueberries for breakfast. Yes, she'd continue, after we swim, let's go down to the garden and get some berries.

Aunt Mollie didn't tolerate a slugabed, and we swam bright and early, before seven o'clock, in a sunken pool lined with flagstones and croaking with morning frogs. I stayed mostly below the surface back then, preferring the cool, pale blue of underwater, but Mollie swam laps back and forth in a careful breast stroke, her gray hair tucked neatly under her swim cap and her head held at a perfect angle to the water, as if she were swimming with a book on her head.

I cannot remember the exact day I tried to eat one of those pears, but I'd guess I was seven or eight and that my aunt was probably having her afternoon lie down. For lunch, we would have sat at the long wooden table and eaten soup made from garden vegetables and served in bowls with round handles. I remember clutching that handle and scooping spoonful after spoonful because the soup was so sweet and peppery and fresh. And because at the scraped bottom of the bowl I'd find an animal—a rooster, a pig, a frog, a horse, or a cow. After soup, we always had Pepperidge Farm cookies, two each, and some more of Aunt Mollie's special iced tea (her secret was using the pestle to grind the sugar into the fresh mint and then soaking it in frozen lemonade). And then it would have been quiet time.

By then, I was probably through all the tiny boxes in the miniature rolltop desk, crayons and postcards and stamps from faraway places, and I was bored. I wasn't allowed outside by myself, and for once I didn't feel like reading. I remember the rich smell of the dark wood and oil in the dining room and how one whole wall was made of glass to look out over the stone patio. The view was out of a fairy tale, sloping down the terraced landscape, ridged with flower beds, and landing at the bottom with a break in the lilies: a shaded opening leading off the stone path to the pool.

All of which reminds me that there's another character in this story: I had a verifiable wicked stepmother. By the age of eight, I'd overheard her telling one of her many sisters on the phone that I was a "little bitch." My stepmother cleaned without ceasing. She's the one who taught me how to make beds with taut hospital corners and then apply the quarter test—if the quarter doesn't bounce on the finished bed, rip out the tucks and begin again. Sometimes she'd be fun, a water balloon fight or a trip out for ice cream, but then she'd switch, fly into a rage, let me know the mint chocolate chip was headed straight for my thighs and I'd better watch it. Summers with my father and stepmother were not happy. I know now that my stepmother's wickedness was the result of mental illness, and I'm guessing this was true for Cinderella and Snow White's as well, but back then, she was just plain mean. All summer long I was sick with nerves; when Aunt Mollie called my father to ask if I could come out and stay for a week, I begged to go and nobody missed me.

So now I want you to try to imagine a bookish girl enjoying a respite away from her distracted father and wicked stepmother, a pair right out of the books, in their city loft that baked in the summer heat. Imagine this girl transported to the cool wood of a shaded heaven, with a kind old lady napping a room away. Imagine how anything might have seemed possible. If there could be a house with chickadees skipping at the windows, bullfrogs croaking in the pond, and trees dropping sour crabapple treats, then a pear made of stone might become real in the right moment. After all, I was a girl who lived at least half my life in books, and I knew that Lucy had stumbled into Narnia through the back of a wardrobe, Mrs. Whatsit had sent Meg and her friends through a wrinkle in time to rescue her father from the planet Camazotz— and Pippi Longstocking? Pippi got to live in her *own* house with a monkey named Mr. Nilsson and a horse named Horse, and she was strong enough to lift them all—house, monkey, and horse— without breaking a sweat. Despite Aunt Mollie's warnings about the fruit, I was convinced of the possibility.

The pear I chose was a model of a Bosc, although I did not know then how to name the lovely neck and buff skin. The convincing indentations on the smooth surface had been carved, and the shading near the stem—a sign of ripeness—had been painted on. The pear felt heavy in my hand, not at all pear-like, certainly not ripe. I must have pressed on the fleshy-looking belly of the pear and met total resistance. My hands should have told me not to bite the pear, so why did I do it? Why would I try to bite a pear I *knew* wasn't real? I don't know, but sitting at my writing desk almost thirty years later—thirty years!—I want to think my failure to read the signs of the physical world had something to do with knowing I was part of a story being written and believing in the possibilities of that story's creation.

I didn't bite down hard, so I didn't hurt my teeth, and despite what we might now read as a failure of possibility, I don't remember feeling at all disappointed, probably because I never hungered for anything when I was at Aunt Mollie's. Not really. I remember my reaction went something like this: Yup. Aunt Mollie is right. This is not a real pear. This pear is a *rock*. Still, I was impressed. So lifelike, that rock pear. So beautiful. I held the pear in my hands, rubbing away my spit, and looked out over the patio and down to the path. I couldn't wait until Aunt Mollie woke up from her nap. We were going down to the garden to pick snap peas for dinner, but first we were stopping by the pond to look for bullfrogs.

In Aunt Mollie's final years the dementia made her paranoid, and she misread the cards I sent in my twenties: thank you, thank you, sweet Mollie, for the magic of early morning swims, leaf tracings, and homemade granola with just-picked blueberries. My notes came too late for her to believe in them, too late for her to know my gratitude was real and full of juice. Saddened, I heard that she read my notes as a ploy for inheritance and that she died trusting no one.

When I was thirteen, I had moved far, far away, all the way across the country to Washington state, and I only saw Aunt Mollie once as an adult, in my early twenties, mere weeks after I'd lost my fiancé in a car accident and instinct told me to go to her. I needed something to believe in again. Most of that final visit is lost to a blur of grief and comfort, but I remember consciously refusing any evidence that the world Mollie created and Mollie herself were more complicated than I'd known them to be. In my mind, perhaps, I wanted to stick to the storybook archetypes of that place and time: kindly fairy godmother rescues miserable child from evil stepmother. A simple story.

Aunt Mollie had made a world where a wounded child could believe in magic, and her mind's final betrayal of her heart seemed to me a cruel irony. In my unprotected girlhood, her home was a place of art and love, a place where a beautiful stone pear refused to yield and still did not disappoint. Her home was an oasis of all things that are good for a child, and the summer weeks that she gave me—could it have been more than a couple of months all together if we strung them end to end?—may have saved my whole life.

Thank you, Aunt Mollie. You were more real than real.

LEADING THE CHILDREN
OUT OF TOWN

When, lo, as they reached the mountain-side,
A wondrous portal opened wide,
As if a cavern was suddenly hollowed;
And the Piper advanced and the children followed,
And when all were in to the very last,
The door in the mountain-side shut fast.

—*The Pied Piper of Hamelin* by Robert Browning

On a bluff above Lake Roosevelt, the streets in my mother's tiny northeastern Washington town are named after apples—Rome Beauty, Northern Spy, Delicious, and so on. Marcus is a magical place, geographically speaking—mountains everywhere you look, and I swear even the clouds are fluffier—but there are few jobs there, no schools, and over a quarter of the families live well below the poverty line.

One summer afternoon, we tucked my one-year-old daughter, Ella, into her stroller and headed out for a walk. A few blocks down the road we passed a yard containing a ride-on toy and a car seat cast by the driveway like a beetle on its back.

The house looked like a place where a child *used* to live, but then a kid Ella's age, maybe a tad older, tumbled out across the stubbly grass wearing gray fleece pajamas and filthy socks. I stopped the stroller, resisting the urge to block this sweet-faced boy from touching my shiny daughter with his grubby hands. He veered to the left, grabbed his rolling toy with both hands, and careened down the sidewalk and into the road.

If this kid had been a *dog*, I would have, at this point, started to look around for his owner. The house he came from was set far back from the road, maybe thirty yards or so, and the curtains were drawn tight.

Gape-mouthed, my mother and I stared at the tumbling baby in the road. He couldn't keep up with the spinning blue wheels, and every six feet or so he tripped on the black scraps of sock dangling at the end of his toes and skidded forward onto his face, but he never cried.

"Be-bee," Ella commented, pointing. "Be-bee."

"Yup," I said. "That's a baby alright. A little baby playing in the street."

We stood there for a while, prepared to run into the street and stop oncoming traffic—Marcus boasts a population of just 160 people, but there is *some* traffic, often teenagers in giant trucks— but no caretaker emerged. The baby made another run at the blue-wheeled toy and lost it again. Again, no tears.

We waited. Ten minutes passed. My mother is quick to defend "different methods," like those of the parents I'd criticized when they pulled up next to our parked car at the laundromat with a toddler and an infant strapped into the back seat, windows rolled up without a crack, both of them smoking. In fact, the smoke was so thick I didn't even *see* the babies until the two adults opened their doors, crushed out their cigarettes, and both walked into the laundromat. I judged the second-hand smoke and the negligence.

My mom hadn't been bothered by either. "Maybe she needed to get her laundry, and she knew it would be easier if the kids waited in the car."

"Mom," I had countered, "there were *two* adults. One of them could have stayed in the car. They were *babies*."

"Well-ll," my mother said, with toe-curling inflection, and ended the conversation. We let it rest with a difference of opinion.

But this time, even my mother was stymied. Here was a toddler, a barely toddling toddler, playing alone in the street. We weren't sure what to do. I suggested we stroll ever so slowly up and down the sidewalk, watching for cars, of course, and always keeping the wordless, running kid close. The baby pushed along behind us with his toy, eyeing Ella.

What I *wanted* to do was march up to the house with the baby in my arms and bang on the door: "Hello? Is this your baby? We found him running in the street. We didn't want him to get hit by a *car* . . ." At this point, the baby had been alone—or, rather, with us, the strange strolling ladies and their own well-padded baby—for fifteen minutes. Then a man with scraggly hair, glasses, and a flannel shirt appeared. He loped out of the house, scowling, and scooped up the kid without a word to us.

This was when I surprised myself. What should I have done? What would *you* have done? Should I have yelled? *You irresponsible freak! You let your kid, your* baby, *play alone in the street?* But I didn't. The moment was so uncomfortable, so weird, a kind of joke came out of my mouth, an excuse for this poor excuse of a father. I laughed, I *laughed*, and I said, "I guess we were kind of like the Pied Piper, leading the children out of town!"

The man didn't answer. He didn't make eye contact. Instead, he swung around and strode back to the house with the kid hanging in his arms like a load of firewood. Maybe he didn't hear me. Maybe he was ashamed. Maybe he didn't know who the fuck the crazy lady with the fancy stroller was talking about. *The Pied friggin' Piper? What the hell.*

Ella lunged forward to get a better look at the disappearing pair, and I checked the five-point safety harness—again—not sure whether to feel responsible, self-righteous, or sad. Pushing Ella away, I thought about the way I cared for my daughter, locking locks and buckling buckles, and how different it was from the way kids were raised where I came from—the way *I* was raised. For reasons I can't quite pin down, this disconnect pissed me off. Was it because in the hormonal flush of my own cautious parenting I rejected this laissez faire approach as nothing short of neglect? Maybe. Or was it because the last I would see of this baby boy—ever—were his feet disappearing into the dark house before the door slammed shut, those blackened socks swinging from the end of his toes like storm-beaten pirate flags.

I know what can happen when kids are left behind, and this knowledge wounds like a cutlass to the heart.

I remember my first Halloween on the mountain when I was thirteen. A trio of men in the holiday spirit piled hay bales and about ten of us kids in the bed of a pickup and bounced us around the mountain to trick-or-treat caramel apples and homemade hot chocolate from far-flung homesteads; when the beer cans of our escorts were empty, they tossed them in the back with the kids and the hay. It was a blast.

We'd moved that year from my childhood home in Massachusetts to an off-the-grid community not too far from Marcus where the primary cash crop was marijuana, and safety precautions were as loose as a dry leaf on a blustery day. As my mother's boyfriend from that time remarked, laughing: "You can't childproof the fuckin' forest. You've got to forestproof the fuckin' kid."

Back then, I owned a thick-coated quarter horse named Moona and rode bareback to our one-room schoolhouse on frigid winter days. In the summer, Moona carried me down to the river, hooves clicking on the shale-covered slopes, and we spent long days alone with the other teenagers and their horses. Sometimes I took her right into the river and clung to her mane, laughing and scared, when she started to swim and the current pushed my thighs up and away from her heaving muscles.

It's true. We mountain kids fended for ourselves, and maybe we're better people for it. Self-sufficient, my mother says. Full of character. Resourceful.

Trust me: these are not parenting strategies I recommend. "It's amazing you survived," my mother says defensively, and I snort in derisive agreement. And yet, most of us did survive. Just like most of the kids on my middle-class street in Muncie, Indiana, survive.

I asked my husband to read an early draft of this essay. I knew I was judging the parents of Marcus—and my own mother—even as I worried I was going all kinds of wrong in the other direction. "You think you're better than they are," Mark said, calling me out.

Do I? Do I tell my Pied Piper story because it makes me feel superior, more confident in the parenting decisions I make every day? Okay, so I fed my kid a hot dog (cut into teeny tiny pieces) for lunch two days in a row, or I plunked her down in front of an extra thirty minutes of *Sesame Street* so I could finish grading a stack of papers. Probably not ideal choices, and yet I can direct attention to this let-the-toddler-play-in-the-street man and say: *Look. Look at him. That's bad, right?*

Goodie for me. Mother of the year.

The man was long gone before I knew what I wanted to tell him. I would have told my mother instead, but she would have said I was exaggerating as usual, being over sensitive, and I didn't need the denigration, the rejection of my rejection. Why am I so intolerant? So *judgmental?*

I said nothing. After the silent man disappeared into the house with the dirty baby, I gripped the padded bar of Ella's stroller and we walked on. There was nothing to see once the door slammed shut. We turned on Minter and then strolled down Jonathan. In the park in the middle of town, ravens complained to us from the tops of the Douglas firs, and chipmunks scattered like tossed pennies into wild rose bushes. Ella was asleep before we reached Rome Beauty and home.

"You know," I could have shouted, "in the original *Pied Piper*, the villagers never saw their children again. They never came out of the cave. They followed him in, and they never came out."

The Pied Piper wasn't the playful, musical clown our cleaned-up editions might suggest. Folklorists date the story's roots as far back as the thirteenth century, and the core tale casts the color-fully dressed Pied Piper as a rat-catcher. In many versions, the Piper leads the rats down to the river, where they drown. But the villagers renege on his full payment, and the Piper returns for the children in retaliation. Sometimes the children are drowned, sometimes led into the cave to be either held captive or killed.

The Pied Piper narrative was constructed to explain something, to use storytelling to find meaning; in this case, a large population of children disappeared in Hamelin, Germany. Nobody knows why. A natural disaster (landslide?), famine, or plague may have wiped them out, and here, the Piper is a figure of death—all fluting metaphor. Or perhaps he is a remaking of a real person who led a kind of Children's Crusade and took the young ones away in a mass emigration.

Psychologists have an unsettling term to describe the capacity of some pedophiles to relate with and seduce children: the Pied Piper effect. This gives me the chills. The reckless freedoms of my own childhood came too soon, and I know this is why my mother's seeming unwillingness to recognize when a child is in danger continues to frustrate me.

As usual, I'm afraid, the story of the careless flannel-shirted man with my Pied Piper framing is really a story about my mother. Not because she was there with me when we found the unsupervised baby but because she did not always protect me when I was a kid.

I forgave her long ago, but I've discovered that forgiveness is something I need to find and offer again and again. Like grief, forgiveness is not a one-time thing. I may also have come to understand why she did what she did when she was raising my brother and me—mostly alone: money was tight, she needed to work, and there was nothing left over for a babysitter even if she'd thought such a precaution was necessary. After all, wasn't my brother around if I wanted something cooked in the oven? "It was a different time," she tells me. "We weren't so aware."

I know what my mother says is true, and she offers this explanation because she's sad. We both know that before we moved to the mountain in Washington when I was thirteen, I was sexually abused by a neighbor, starting when I was just six or seven. I have healed. I can love and be loved. As a teenager, I was pretty messed up, but now I am better—mostly.

My daughter, Ella, a baby in this story, just turned seven. I look at her perfect forty-eight-pound body, stretched out in sleep, lightly concealed by thin white ballerina pajamas dotted with tiny pink hearts, and I can't imagine. The horror. Ella is the reason I keep returning to the story of the running child. She is so beautiful. When I tiptoe into her room at night to check on her and see her sleeping in the crack of light that shines out of her closet to help her feel safe—she has never liked complete darkness— her innocence stops my breath. The Pied Piper story, in the end, reminds me of the girl in me who never made it out of the cave. She's back there still. When she was set loose in the street in her dirty socks, no well-meaning strangers happened upon her to block the random chance of an approaching truck. Her mother is at work, she's on the top bunk of her bed, and there's a much older boy slipping his rough hands under the covers to touch her. She doesn't speak. He does what he will do, and she keeps their shared secret.

Rejecting the tyranny of silence, I have told the story of this abuse. The secret is out. My mother knows and she is sorry. She is terribly, terribly sorry. She laments that she cannot go back and change this scene.

What would I have my mother do? I guess I want her to agree with me about the babies left alone in the smoky car at the laundromat. I want her to point a judgmental finger at the flannel-shirted father of the baby in the street. I don't want her to accept these displays of neglect as "different methods." I need her to join me in my righteous anger.

But that's not the kind of woman my mother is, and anyway, maybe there's nothing to be done. Maybe this is something my mother and I live with between us, with my anger rising up unbidden and randomly, like a sharp thistle in the garden of our deep affection. I guess that's okay. And maybe the girl in the cave is not so much a whole girl but a ghost girl, a simulacrum still gritting her angry teeth.

Maybe I can't scoop the girl I was out of the dark cave with all her living parts any more than my mother can make that trip back in time to save her before it's too late, but I can let her and all the children like her know that I remember. I can use her story to protect my own sweet Ella and others I find along the way who might need someone big to stand between them and danger, and maybe, if I keep telling and telling, I can use her story to pry open the side of that sealed-up mountain, releasing the lost children into the light.

SLAUGHTERHOUSE ISLAND

The thing about telling this story even thirty years later is that even though I know where the culpability rests—firmly—I have trouble soaking off the most dogged shame. I am scraping away the last of the sticky residue with my thumbnail.

Yes, I did some stupid things. We all do. But now I know we're allowed to be kids who mask our gut-deep insecurities with vanity. We get to wear crop-tops and tight jeans with a ribbon of lace for a belt and high-heeled boots. We get to check ourselves thirty times in the dorm-room mirror, necks craning to see how fat our skinny little asses look from the back, and we even get to guzzle sweet drinks and swallow harmless-looking tabs we hope might make us feel better or dance faster or look prettier or just forget. We get to want something to come easy for a change. We get to make every choice on that daily life scale from forward-thinking to utter self-sabotage.

And we still don't deserve to be raped.

How did we ever get to a place where victim-blaming is wedged so far into our brains? *Turn this around*, I think to myself, scraping with my thumbnail. *Turn this around. What would Kurt have had to do for me to feel justified in raping him?*

There's no answer to that question.

I want to fold time. I want to walk into that Italian restaurant in Eugene, Oregon, where my eighteen-year-old self is having her first awkward date with Kurt, take her by the hand, and ask her to join me in the bathroom. Instead of letting her throw up the four bites of creamy pasta she ate for dinner—which I know is all she can really think about as she watches Kurt's pointy teeth flash in the candlelight—I want to pull her around the corner, hurry down the hall in the opposite direction, and make for the exit.

We'll leave together, I'll walk her back to the dorm, and we'll have a talk. I'll save her, somehow, from what's going to happen to us next, even though, sweet girl, I know it's not her fault. *None of this was ever your fault. Do you hear me? Not. Your. Fault.*

But from here, back in the future, I can only watch.

"You drive a Porsche"—rhyming with "borscht" without the final "t"—I'd said after I'd lowered myself down onto the soft leather of Kurt's sleek silver car, hoping my friends on the second floor of the freshman dorm were peeking from behind the curtains. He'd leaned in toward me, breath too minty, already-thinning dark hair glinting with product in the spring sunshine, and moved his large hand from the gearshift to my thigh. I think he was trying to look sexy but managed instead to look maniacal.

"Por-shhhha," he said. "People who don't have Por-shas call them Porsches. People who *drive* Por-shas call them Por-shas."

I moved my knee a fraction, the tiniest of objections, and said, "Well, *I* don't have a Porsche, so I'd better call it a Porsche."

"You're with me now," he said, thin lips curling into a smile. "Now you can call this car a Por-sha."

I hadn't had a date like this before—what I imagined to be a real college date, during which Kurt picked up, moved, or lifted everything that might need picking up, moving, or lifting: the door to the Por-sha, my chair at the table, my body by the arm when another man came too close, and of course, the check. We went to a real, sit-down Italian restaurant with white linen tablecloths, candles, and dim lighting, where we talked about the extensive time he and I both spent at the gym on the edge of campus: me in aerobics classes burning away any calories I'd consumed in moments of weakness, and he lifting and slamming giant iron discs in the testosterone soup that was the main gym.

We were both too tan, this being the era of ten tans for twenty dollars in the warm booths on the campus strip. I was in my first year in the Honors College, reading Darwin and Shakespeare and Austen, having my mind blown by Mary Shelley's *Frankenstein* and theories about sexual selection and how the universe began. Kurt was in business, a supersenior—the first I'd heard such a moniker, though it didn't take me long to figure out that the "super" didn't mean anything good.

Since we had nothing else to discuss, the conversation turned to tanning. I told him how I always fell asleep under the lights, the humming blue womb offering respite from the gray Eugene winter—although I'm sure I wouldn't have said "womb," not that night—and Kurt's teeth glowed in the dim candlelight like something out of a horror movie.

After dinner, Kurt took me back to an apartment that looked like nobody lived there, gave me something to drink, and led me through the living room with its black leather couch and glass coffee table into his bedroom. Closing the door behind him, he showed me the hand weights he kept in a line by the wall, like shoes, and then pushed me toward a desk. I remember his hands always on my body, and even before he pulled the mirror and the razor blade out of the center drawer, I was thinking, *This isn't good.*

Kurt reached into the pocket of his coat and pulled out a paper packet—druggie origami—tapping two snowy piles onto the glass. I watched him chopping and scraping, wincing a bit at the sound, a fork on china, nails on a chalkboard, a warning alarm I would fail to heed. Down to the roots of my nerve fibers, I knew the thing to do was get out, but this was to be a night of many college firsts: first restaurant date, first ride in a Porsche, first blow. Kurt rolled a crisp green bill from his wallet and showed me what to do.

It burned. And then? Not much. The coke had done nothing more than make my eyes feel really, really wide open. I would be hyperalert for what came next.

Which was also almost nothing. He kissed me, and as he did, he pulled me away from the desk and down onto the bed. He was the world's worst kisser, all probing tongue, like a sea slug trying to move down my throat. I was repulsed but saved (I know now) by the coke: Kurt couldn't get it up. He rolled against me, and through the thin fabric of his dress khakis, I could feel him against my thigh, soft as a dinner roll.

George Michael sang through the speakers. Rather than pursue what he must have known from experience was a losing game, Kurt sprang from the bed, as if he'd planned it that way, and went to the stereo to turn it up. *I will be your father figure.* Thirty minutes later, when I asked for a ride back to the dorm, he gave me one without much of a fight. In the Por-sha.

The next day, apparently having had more fun than I had, Kurt called to ask if I'd go with him to Shasta Lake, an annual Memorial Day fraternity tradition at the University of Oregon: at least a hundred rented houseboats, each carrying eight or so couples, kegs tapped and flowing, red Silo cups bobbing in the water like buoys.

Imagine the drinking and the drugs. Imagine the sleeplessness and the young, unfinished brains. Imagine the heat, the dehydration, and the food packed by the boy-men hosting this nightmare. Imagine that nobody on the whole boat had the sense to bring sunscreen. Imagine the depth of seething, unmet need—and then imagine the depth of the water.

Imagine, too, that I'd already made plans to go with a friend from my dorm, a guy named Jeff, who had pledged a fraternity the previous fall. Stretched to his full height, Jeff reached only to my nose, but he was clever and made me laugh, so when he'd quite casually offered to bring me along to Shasta, I'd agreed.

But a real invitation from a real date with a real car and a real apartment with real furniture seemed like just the kick in status I needed to go from full-scholarship hippie kid with Beatles posters and batik bedspreads stapled to the walls of her dorm room to . . .

to what? What did I want to be? Part of the system my liberal, artist parents had always rejected? Noticed? Accepted? Desired?

I didn't even like Kurt. He represented everything I'd been taught to distrust in the world—a privileged fuck from the Portland burbs who thought anything could be his for the right price, including me.

So, at first, I did the right thing: I said no to Kurt. But my best girlfriend, Jenny, had *not* gotten a date for the lake trip, and I felt bad leaving her behind. Also, I didn't want to go on this trip as a lone independent—an Honors College student, a veritable freak—in a vast Grecian sea, with Jeff as my sole companion. So when Kurt's frat buddy agreed to take Jenny on the trip with us if I would go with Kurt, I consented.

And then all hell broke loose.

When I told Jeff that I was going with Kurt instead, he flipped out. His room was just below mine, and all night he played angry music and hung out his window screaming that I was a bitch, a whore, a fucking cunt. Other boys from the dorm joined Jeff in his righteous fury, smashing things against the floor, pounding on my door, and hissing through the crack.

I didn't get mad back. I felt terrible and guilty, cowering in my room while the whole male population of my dorm rose up with a clear message: I had belonged to them and I had strayed from the pack, hooking up with a rogue male and threatening the sanctity of the whole goddamned dormitory gene pool. All night I took in their anger, crying so hard and so long without the good sense to take out my contact lenses that, in the morning, I had to have an emergency appointment with the ophthalmologist. My corneas were both scratched, one so badly I had to wear an eye patch.

I was a sea wench who had survived the shaming, but barely. And there was no turning back now. I would go to Shasta as a pirate, with Kurt.

We hadn't even left the dock before it was obvious that Jenny's companion wasn't much of a date—they weren't even speaking to each other—but she didn't care. She may as well have been on another boat, lost as she was in drugs, Jack Daniels, and the eyes of a new friend with whom she was swaying near a boom box, hitting rewind on a worn Eagles cassette, "Desperado" locked in as their song. By the time Kurt and his pack of drunken brothers, baked in every way there is to be baked, anchored our boat on Slaughterhouse Island in the middle of Shasta Lake, the deep water was not just a metaphor.

On the roof deck in my magenta bikini, I felt alone and trapped. The fraternity brothers on the boat assigned all the girls nicknames for the weekend, and mine—because of my big rib cage, some gruesome predatory reference to dead meat, or something else I'll never know—was *Carcass*. Kurt hovered over me.

I knew it was too late to get away, and somehow, I knew what was coming.

I don't know how many white houseboats docked on our side of the island that night—at least a dozen. After the sun had set, fires sprang up, the music got louder, and voices rose in a discordant roar. I'd refused the coke all day—that night in Kurt's apartment had been enough for me—but when the party was raging, Kurt pulled a baggie out of his pocket and held something out to me in the palm of his big hand. Brown mushrooms like shrunken heads on tiny necks. I took a few and chewed the tough, dry stems, washing them down with a slug from his beer.

When the mushrooms started to kick in, I slipped away from Kurt and the hordes of drunken Greeks, climbing the bare slope where the dark, swaying shapes of human bodies circled the flames, pushing through some thick brush near the top, and finding shelter next to what seemed at the time to be a fantastically magnanimous scrub pine.

From my refuge, I watched the bonfires burning red, a postapocalyptic hellscape, the moored houseboats bobbing like a flotilla of crocodiles. I was well hidden, and far below I could see Kurt moving from boat to boat to boat, up and down the bank, looking for me, screaming my name, yelling, "Where is she? Where the fuck is she? Who's she with? Who'd you see her with?"

I was with nobody, alone on top of the hill, and I knew when I came down, I would be caught, so I stayed under the tree: two o'clock, three o'clock, four o'clock. The mushrooms wore off, and I was tired—so tired and so cold. When I finally didn't see him anymore, I crept back down to the boat.

This was my thought: *If I am in bed, if I am in bed and sleeping when he finds me, maybe he will let me sleep. I will sleep until tomorrow when the boat will return to the dock, and I will be safe.* But when he found me, I was not safe.

They will wake you up to rape you.

The next morning, when the boat docked, Kurt walked up into town and came back with a bag of Dunkin' Donuts—cream filled, jelly filled, powdered, and plain, at least two dozen—and he said to me, "Here, Jill. You get first choice."

Six hours before, he'd had a pillow stuffed in my mouth to muffle my screams, and now he had the nerve to give me first choice on a bag of fucking doughnuts.

I wondered then if I could have fought harder—I hadn't bitten off his earlobe and spit it in his face, I hadn't jammed my knee into his testicles with all the force of my starved eighteen-year-old body, I hadn't leaped to my feet and rammed a well-placed heel into his kneecap. I pleaded, I cried, and finally I screamed for help, but I didn't hurt him back because I didn't want to die.

I remember the pillow in my face and, when there wasn't air enough left for screaming, thinking *breathe, breathe, breathe.*

In the bright morning sun, Kurt looked hideous, the bag of doughnuts hanging in the air between us, the smell of hot sugar over stale beer and vomit all around us. His eyes registered nothing, nothing at all, and I imagined clawing them out.

"No, thank you," I said, turning away. "I don't eat doughnuts."

When we got back from California, Kurt called me on the dorm phone in the hall, again and again. Here's what I didn't say: "You fucker. You *raped* me. You think I'm going to *go out* with you?"

Here's what I did say: "I'm busy," and "I can't," and "I have to work/write a paper/do some math."

I didn't call what happened on the boat that weekend *rape*.

And then, a month after Shasta, I agreed to see Kurt.

I had a ticket out of Portland to fly to Savannah, Georgia, and I needed a ride to the airport. Kurt wanted to be that ride. *What harm could come of it?* I thought. Some nice boys from the Honors College—actual friends—got me as far as Portland and offered at least ten times to take me from the bookstore where we were hanging out to the airport. They didn't know what Kurt had done to me, but they knew I didn't like him.

Why did I let Kurt come and pick me up? I still can't answer that question.

"Jill! It's so good to see you," Kurt said when he pulled up to where I was standing by the curb with my suitcase. "I've missed you. Have you missed me?" He tried to kiss me, but I turned my face away. Kurt unlatched the tiny trunk, wedged in my suitcase, and then, putting his hand on the small of my back, guided me to the passenger's side of the growling car.

As soon as I was in, I noticed something hanging from the rearview mirror. Something familiar.

"Hey," I said. "That's mine."

"Yes," Kurt said, touching a finger to the loop of white lace knotted around the base of the mirror. "Your belt. I wanted something to remember you by."

I reached up to snatch down Kurt's trophy, but he stopped my hand and squeezed, leering. "Finder's keepers."

As the Porsche pulled away from the curb, I felt a wave of loathing and fear.

Kurt took the wrong road out of downtown, heading west instead of north. "Where are you going?" I asked.

"I forgot something at my parents' place," he said. "We're just going to swing by on our way to the airport."

"But it's not *on* the way to the airport." I knew Kurt was living with his parents in the suburbs.

"It's fine," he said, grinning. "You've got plenty of time."

At the house, I wanted to wait in the car, but he said I should come in to meet his parents. They weren't home, of course, and somehow we ended up in Kurt's bedroom. He closed the door.

"What are you doing?" I said. "I have to go!"

Kurt put his face close to my face, the aftershave, the mint, all of him sickening to me. We were in a kind of dance, me backing up until I hit the edge of the bed. Kurt smiled.

He put his hands on my shoulders and pushed me down. I landed flat on my back, and he fell over me, pinning me down with his body.

Again. No. Nononono. It was going to happen again.

Then we heard something, someone coming in the door.

Kurt jumped off me and reached down, offering me his hand and pulling me up. I was in shock. I said nothing. There was nothing left for me to say.

Kurt laughed. "What did you think I was going to do, Jill? Rape you?"

In his own terrifying way, Kurt had named his own crime before I could, and yet I never filed a report. I never even said, "You raped me." I did nothing. I got out of that fucking car at the airport, and I never saw him again.

In the bunk on Shasta Lake, Kurt had put a pillow over my face so no one would hear me scream, but now I wonder: *Who would have heard me?* And if someone had heard, on that boat anchored to an island I didn't know until today was named for an actual meat market and slaughterhouse, would they have acted? Who would have helped me? From the distance of nearly thirty years, my heart made vulnerable by motherhood and my fierce desire to protect my children, I wonder, *How many other women were raped that night on Slaughterhouse Island?*

I feel certain I was not the only one.

In Savannah the summer after the rape, I had sex with more different men in three months than in all the years before and all the years after combined. My then-unarticulated logic went like this: if I give my body away, over and over, I can prove to myself that sex is my choice—even though, and this seems significant now, I always let the men choose me. Until I was nineteen years old, it never occurred to me that I could do the choosing. *Not you, not you, not you. Yes, okay. You.*

The morning I wrote this essay, I went to my bookshelf and hooked a finger over the red spine of a paperback: *I Never Called It Rape.* The cover is designed to look as if part of the book has been ripped away, and the pages of my copy are browning on the edges. Published in 1988, the very year I went to Shasta with Kurt, reporter Robin Warshaw's book revealed the results of Mary Koss's *Ms.*/NIMH-funded survey. Theirs was the first nationwide study of campus sexual assault ever, and the statistics rattled us all: *Twenty-five percent of women in college have been the victims of rape or attempted rape. Eighty-four percent of these victims were acquainted with their assailants. Only 27 percent of women raped identified themselves as rape victims.*

I bought the book as a sophomore, when it was a required text for a class called "Self-Defense from the Inside Out." *Holy shit*, I thought then. *Why didn't anybody tell me this before?*

Here, in the pages of *I Never Called It Rape*, I can have a conversation with my college self: she wrote—not a lot—in purple pen, scratching asterisks next to the things that mattered most to her. *One in four female respondents had an experience that met the legal definition of rape or attempted rape* and *The average age when a rape incident occurred (either as perpetrator or victim) was 18½ years old* and *[Women] were embarrassed about the details of the rape (leaving a bar with a man, taking drugs, etc.) and felt they would be blamed for what occurred, or they simply felt the men involved had too much social status for their stories to be believed* and *In short, many men fail to perceive what has just happened as rape.*

"The question," our self-defense teacher said one afternoon when we were gathered around her cross-legged on mats in the gym, "is not 'What will he think of me?'—if I don't answer his question, if I'm not polite, if I don't want to go—but 'What do I think of *him?*'"

This simple rearrangement of pronouns flipped something in my brain. Forever.

"If a guy on the street approaches you and asks for the time," our teacher said, "you don't have to answer him. Providing the time of day is not your job. If you don't want to talk to him, keep walking."

You don't have to be polite. You don't even have to be nice. Keep walking.

Ask yourself: What do I think of *him?*

Three years after the rape, I began volunteering at a local sexual assault support organization, staffing the crisis line and going with a team to talk to high school students about rape. In 1991 conversations about what constituted true consent were still new, and while the boys sat silently, the girls pushed back. "So you're saying that if I go to a party in a really short skirt, and I'm flirting all over the place—if I get raped, it's not my fault?"

"Yes," I'd respond. "That's exactly what I'm saying." Sometimes it seemed to me that the girls just didn't want to hear that rape is never the victim's fault. They wanted to have something to believe in, rules to follow, a formula, reasons other girls got raped and they didn't: short skirt equals rape; too much beer equals rape; unlocked door equals rape. The part I wanted them to understand is that these equations can implode, constricting your whole life, until one day you're sitting in a locked steel box breathing through an air hole with a straw and wondering, *Now? Now am I safe?*

A couple months before the rape, a truck had hit me. It wasn't a big truck—one of those little ones, a Toyota or a Nissan with a canopy on the back. I was riding across the crosswalk on my bike. I knew I was supposed to walk my bike across, but I had the green light and the white walking man, so I had started to zip across when the man driving the truck, not seeing me, made the decision to turn right on red. I went down hard, but I was wearing a helmet, and though the truck didn't stop right away, it did soon enough. My legs and half my twisted bike were under the bumper. When I wriggled free, I felt nothing in particular until I saw the horrified, worried face of the man emerging from the cab and the two women running from the building across the street. "Oh my God, are you okay? Are you okay?" A car stopped behind the truck. Lying on the cold, wet road, I was surrounded by concerned bystanders. I did feel something then: mortification and shame.

My arm and leg on the pavement side were both bleeding. I wasn't dressed for the weather or for biking. I was coming back from a class at the gym, so I was wearing a sweatshirt and black Lycra pants. *Ruined now*, I thought. *Shit.*

"Are you okay?" Everybody seemed to be saying the same thing, over and over, and I was worried they were all going to get really wet. It was March in Eugene, with drizzle so thick and gray and constant I couldn't tell whether the raindrops were moving up or down.

I must have been in shock.

"Are you okay?"

"Yeah," I mumbled, grabbing for the bumper and pulling myself off the ground. Hands all around, but I reached out for none of them. "I'm fine. I'm okay."

Somehow we all got to the sidewalk on the other side. My bike had a twisted rim and was unrideable.

"Are you sure you're okay? Can we help you get somewhere?"

"Oh, no, I'm fine. My dorm's right over there. I'm fine."

And so everybody left, even the little truck that had flattened me, and I thought over and over: *I feel like I've been run over by a truck*. In fact, I *had* been run over by a truck, but I couldn't say that out loud. I couldn't say how much it hurt. Embarrassed of being in the wrong place at the wrong time in the wrong pants, I limped back to my dorm in the rain.

Do you understand yet why we blame ourselves when we are hit, dragging the shame behind us like a twisted rim?

In 2014 psychologists at the University of Oregon conducted the first comprehensive, university-wide survey on sexual assault and learned that 19 percent of female students are victims of rape or attempted rape during the time they're studying at Oregon.

Nineteen percent. One in five women.

I am still scraping at my story. I can't go back and get the young woman I was from the Italian restaurant before she climbs onto the boat. I can't stop the truck or the rapist, but I can let the girl I was know that I see her. I hear her. I know she is telling the truth.

If nothing changes—and in thirty years, not nearly enough has changed—next year, there will be one hundred thousand more assaults on our campuses.

In the self-defense class, our teacher taught us that if we couldn't imagine doing something—cracking an assailant in the head with a stapler, opening up a can of pepper spray on an attacker, digging our keys into the eyes of a would-be rapist—we wouldn't be able to act in a real crisis. Wielding the stapler, the pepper spray, and the keys, our teacher taught us the power of visualization, and I learned to imagine in advance what I might be called upon to do in an emergency.

One hundred thousand? This is an emergency.

Together, let's visualize what we need to do to turn this motherfucking system around. I have my keys in my hand, and I am holding them like a claw.

PART III

And death i think is no parenthesis

THE AVOCADO

If the answer was the smooth brown pit at the center of a ripe avocado I bought for breakfast from the man on the corner in San Jose, Costa Rica, then the question began with the slippery green nubs on the surface, the ones I ran my thumb across for courage as I walked back to my single bed in the pension, past a group of men on the street, all of them hissing *que guapa que guapa que guapa*. Twenty years old, blue-eyed and dark-haired, I didn't know my own beauty, would never have thought to consider such a phrase—*my own beauty*—but I held a growing sense of my body's place at the center of things. I mean this in a geological way: the shifting and slipping of solids and liquids, the crunching of plates, the obliteration of the eruption, and afterward, the layering, the building up.

At home in Oregon, before the tow truck hit my fiancé's van in the cold November of the previous year, I wore tight sweaters, white cowboy boots, snug jeans with a thin ribbon of lace around my too-small waist. Before the accident made Colin's body something they wouldn't even let me see, never mind touch, I still counted catcalls on my walk from the yogurt shop to my Shakespeare class, but I had a dawning understanding that my heart's acceleration in the electric heat from strangers on the street was more fear than power, more "fuck you" than fun.

This tectonic shift may be partially credited to my first women's studies class, but the real change came from the way Colin loved me. Of course he loved my body, as I loved his, but he also loved *me.* I'd been having sex since my midteens and before that, when I was a child—a bedrock violation, my body the property of our neighbor across the field long before I knew it was mine. Before Colin, I'd held all that down, buried deep, not knowing how much work I had to do before my body was mine—bones and flesh, skin and hair, hard parts and soft parts—a body I could share if I wanted, without giving anything away.

It makes sense, then, that the teenage sex I had before Colin was like something I watched on TV—not all bad, sometimes comical, never better than a book, but always from a distance, always from the other side of a screen. Before Colin, I didn't stay in my body for sex. I slipped out, a curl of steam, a wisp of vapor, and no one seemed to notice I was gone. Not even me. But Colin loved me enough to know this, and we practiced. He'd watch for my departure, and if something pulled me away, he would stop whatever he was doing and lie next to me holding my hand. Together we were safe and together we could burn.

In the single year we had together, Colin beckoned me down from the walls, back from the edges, to inhabit my body, a real woman's body. With his fingers, his tongue, the firm pressure of all of him, he walked the ledge of my collarbone, fed the curved lines of my ribs, and kissed—again and again—the freckled birthmark spreading across the top third of my left thigh. In the middle school dressing room, the mean girls had pointed, calling out my *dirty spot*, heckling me to *wash off the mud*, but Colin saw something else. "Look," he said, turning my hip with his palm. "A lion. She's running, looking over her shoulder." And I could see her there. *Yes.* Together, we roared, and then Colin took his own body and went away. He saved my life, and then he died.

On the day of that perfect avocado, I was four months into a kind of volcanic winter, the sun occluded by the ash that rose up when Colin had burned, when his strong, golden, six-foot-two body—so beautiful—had become something the man in the side room at the funeral home could hand to me in a small cardboard box.

I remember being surprised by the weight, the muscles in my arms tightening to pull him to my chest, feeling the heat in the box when the ashes shifted. *No. No.*

Now what?

Sliding down the continent on a black wash of grief, I hid my diminished self in a shapeless dress, the line falling straight and loose from top to bottom, my skin untouched except the top of my well-covered breasts and my shins, tickled by the cotton hem with each stride, bright orange poppies on pale blue backing. I marched straight lipped and eyes ahead through the path the men cleared, holding my avocado in both hands like a gift. I wondered if they could read my sad story in my eyes.

What if I stopped and told them? What if I handed one of them my avocado and he whipped a blade from his back pocket to carve the fruit into trembling green slices to share? What if I let him lay one on my tongue?

Still hissing, the men stepped back, parting the waters of their male bodies, and I moved through. Nobody touched me, not even a brush of my dress, and I didn't stop walking. I didn't even look. *Too much color*, I thought. *Orange poppies are a reckless choice for a grieving girl.* I kept moving, stroking the hide on my avocado, my own skin rippling like a horse shooing a fly with a tremor of flesh. *Que guapa sssssssssssssssss.* The men were not aggressive, or even unkind. They sent me around the corner to the heavy wooden door of my pension with more words I couldn't understand then and cannot remember now.

But I remember the way the loneliness of that narrow bed shifted when I palmed the avocado, my alligator pear, pressing my knife into the tough skin until the tip plunged through flesh, knocking against the pit as if against a door. Hearing no answer, just the communal shower through the thin wall, I pulled the blade around the equator until she fell open, divided, onto the clear plastic bag I'd laid out as a placemat.

The flesh inside was perfect, almost too beautiful to eat. Avocado green is not, in fact, the desexed color of 1970s stand mixers but something more complicated, a gradation of shade from buttercream near the nut-brown pit to deep-shade-in-the-forest green at the perimeter where flesh meets frame. On one hemisphere, the clinging brown pit glowed gold, a cross-sectioned woman, heavy with child. On the other side, a hollow, a vacancy, a curvature where something vital had been but was now gone.

I ate that shadowed side first. After color, texture is all, and the merchant on the corner with his basket and I in my traveling dress had captured our fruit in that closing window when my plastic spoon could slip through the flesh to scoop morsels like ice cream not too long out of the freezer: yielding but firm, so deliciously transient.

Colin had been dead for one season—a single winter—and here was a succulent loneliness I could hold on my tongue, a sensuality I could take in.

Stay here, I ordered myself. *Don't go.*

The accident happened at a crossroads in Tillamook, a small town on the coast of Oregon most famous today for cheddar cheese. What's notable about Tillamook historically is also the thing that brought Colin and his workmates, all young men, to the dark crossroads where they died that night: during World War II, the navy built the two largest free-standing wooden structures in the world in Tillamook, hangars massive enough to play six games of football simultaneously—in each one. On that soggy day in November, Colin and his friends had been in one of those giant hangars preparing a Virgin lightship for the next day's planned inflation. The blimps were a pet project of British entrepreneur Richard Branson, extreme adventurer and would-be knight. I don't blame Branson for what happened to Colin, but whenever I hear about his high-risk exploits in balloons or speedboats or spaceships, I think: *Sir Richard, were the brakes good on that company van? Was your guy okay to drive? Did you leave some men behind on life's big adventure?*

Twenty-four years later, Colin has been dead longer than the twenty-two years he was alive, I am old enough to be *mother* to the young man he was when he died, and the scope of that perspective looks to me like a cavernous, wood-framed building, a wonder of engineering and the last structure Colin ever stood in, a space big enough to fly a jet plane through. Three young men died that night, two British and one American—Colin—and a second American survived, diminished. I wonder now if they felt small in that looming, covered air, or whether the sense of sheer enormity—I remember Colin stretching his long arms, fingers up and open, as if he were trying to carry a cloud, trying to explain to me the size, the *hugeness*—made these young men feel bigger, more invincible, as they climbed into the minivan, not bothering with seatbelts, and headed down the road for a pizza.

It makes me sad to know they died hungry.

In the days after the phone call came in, I couldn't eat and I couldn't stop vomiting. I maintain only flickers of memory from these first weeks, but I remember the ginger snaps. With Colin's sisters and brothers and parents all around me, numb or wailing or rocking in the lava flow of deep grief—of seven children, Colin had been the baby, their *baby*—I know I wasn't the only one who needed something I could swallow, but my recollection is that the ginger snaps were brought home especially for me. Why can't I remember any faces? Why can I better remember the yellow box of dry, round cookies than the decimated family who tried to feed me?

The psychiatrist at my school had called in a prescription for suppositories to calm me down, stop the vomiting, and put me to sleep. But I wasn't using them faithfully. I wanted to be awake if Colin visited me in the night. I was a shattered body waiting for one that had been burned to dust. I wanted to follow him, but someone (my mother? Colin's mother? his sister?) broke off a piece of ginger snap and made me stick out my tongue. The fragment of wafer stuck there. I pulled in my tongue like a toad, hoping they could now let me die.

There are other parts of the story that seem to matter, although I'm not sure where they fit in, how to tell them. When we drove to Tillamook to pick up Colin's ashes, we stopped by the crossroads where he died, and I thought, *This is the last place Colin was alive. I am standing where Colin took his last breath.* In the dirt, I found a fragment of mirror. I can't remember if we went to the crossroads on the day of the funeral home, or if they wouldn't let me then, if I drove back to Tillamook later, alone. I know I went back. Now I can see the intersection of Highway 101 and Long Prairie Road on Google Maps. I can swoop down to street level and with a stroke of my finger turn my gaze, surprised by the blow to the gut, startling myself by thinking, still: *This is the last place Colin was alive. I am standing where Colin took his last breath.*

In 1992, three years after the accident, there was a fire in Hangar A. Apparently, they'd been using the giant blimp structure to store hay, lots of hay—7,600 tons of dry tinder. Fifteen fire engines rushed to the scene, and unable to enter the burning building, seventy firefighters stood in the dark, faces glowing, and watched one of the two largest free-span wooden structures in the world burn to the ground.

It must have been spectacular. A conflagration to beat all conflagrations.

We drove with Colin's ashes to the ranch in northern California where he'd played with his dogs and learned to catch calves. We made a mound of him on a hill, almost a sand castle. When the rest of the family stumbled back to the barn for the pancake breakfast, they let me stay with Colin, my mind frantic. I was on my knees. What could I do? What now?

Here is what I did: I sprinkled some ashes into my palm, thick, grainy, with pieces of bone, and I kissed them. I licked him from my lips, felt him crunch between my teeth. I told him to stay with me. I explained my sudden plan, an inspiration: "I am taking you into me."

Stay with me. Don't go.

In slow spoonfuls, on my bed in the pension, I ate only half of the avocado and wrapped the other in the plastic bag to save, knowing that where the pit touched the flesh, the enzymes would preserve the green. I wasn't traveling alone in Costa Rica, but I usually *was* alone. My traveling companions were also grieving, and we had trouble finding each other in our separate fogs. Colin's brother, the one with the same olive skin and deep brown eyes but ten years older, was there for the same reason I was—to escape his grief, or walk through it and into the rainforest's center. His girlfriend was there, too, but on the day I'd flown in, they'd broken up, and she was grieving the loss of her own little brother—murdered. I came to realize their parallel pain was the one and only thing that could have brought these two opposing forces together even for a night. She despised me. She hated me for being young, making disgusted noises in her throat and tossing her dusty blond hair like a weapon when we passed the desk of the pension together and the young clerk watched me the way he always did, moist-eyed and trembling.

On the day of the avocado, I told the clerk at the desk—who had become my friend—about the men and their hissing. He smiled longingly and said in his perfect English: "No, no, señorita. They don't mean to scare you or insult you. They want to give you a compliment. They want to tell you that you are beautiful. That's all. Take their compliment and be happy. Be happy, señorita."

That afternoon we boarded a bus north to see Arenal, the always-smoking volcano. We traveled on so many buses for so many hours and it was so many years ago, I'm not confident I can pick this day out from all the others. I know it takes at least three hours to get to Arenal from San Jose. I want to say there was rain that day, and that we boarded a more modern bus with high-backed, individual, Greyhound-style seats for the first leg before getting dropped off during an afternoon storm in a little town where I drank an icy Orange Crush from a thick glass bottle, standing with my back against the wall while the heavy rain sluiced off the awning and splashed my sandaled toes. When the next bus finally came, it was bench-seated, like a school bus, and we bounced the rest of the way.

For once, there was no dust. The rain had wet down the road to the volcano. I felt for my avocado through the nylon on my waist pack to make sure it was not getting smashed. Everything that touched my body—the warm tin siding on my back, the smooth bottle on my lips, the hard seat against my thighs, my own reaching hand on my belly near the avocado—made me think of Colin.

No body to feel another day's touches. No body to touch my body. No body.

Half a lifetime ago, on the bus to Arenal, I couldn't yet know how this body of mine would rise up in grief's heat, a collision of continental and oceanic plates, the solid I could touch, holding me together, and the liquid that was most of me, bubbling, carrying me along through another twenty years in my changing form from grieving girl to lover, lover, lover, then wife, then mother, my baby girl thriving, then grieving again—the new baby in my womb damaged, my body opened up to take him out, my body the site of our loss and grief, my body the scene of the accident, my whispered prayer to Colin: "Please take care of my baby. Keep him warm. Don't let him go hungry."

After the surgery that removed our son from my womb, I wondered how my husband would ever touch me again without thinking about what we'd made together, imperfectly, and then lost, with that same crashing together of human imperfection. More loss, more bleeding, and then another birth, a living son to join our daughter, all of us waiting and wanting, and me lying in our huge bed, nursing my new baby boy, thinking: *How will I ever be grateful enough for my body and what she has done?*

When we finally arrived, I sat alone on a log by the lake with my avocado, savoring my last bites with sputtering Arenal rising up before me. She was like a volcano from a science fair, hand-shaped with clay by eager hands into a perfect cone. She was quintessential, the platonic ideal, all of us imperfect in her smoking shadow.

After so many disappointments, Arenal was the volcano I expected her to be.

Licking the buttery green from my spoon, I looked down and noticed an astounding line of leafcutter ants carrying bright, freshly cut leaves in their mandibles. Swaying past in the current of their own community, the shiny ants looked like catamarans with outsized sails. I'd missed the beginning of the line and would never see the end. I took pity, and after scraping the avocado clean I put the shell in the ants' path, hoping my clean would be their idea of feast, an avocado cruise, but the ants diverted their line, like green water around a rock, and kept moving, unfazed and unwavering, eyes ahead.

I meant only to be kind, to offer the only thing I had to give.

Arenal is all woman. She's a composite volcano, which means that she's built herself up in layers of hardened lava and pumice and ash, explosion after explosion, holding her magma deep in her core until she can't any longer. Until she loses it. And then even her spewed rage and grief and sorrow harden, make her bigger.

Arenal rose up because of what the seismologists call convergence. In her case, an oceanic plate colliding with a continental plate, with no place to go but up.

In 1990, when I was there with my avocado, Arenal had been steaming and spewing daily since a summer afternoon in 1968 when, after four centuries of quiet dormancy, she blew, burning three villages and killing eighty-seven villagers. Having come into her power, Arenal kept it up for thirty years, until a day in May 1998 when she erupted twenty-three times in a single afternoon and then gave up her daily venting.

In the seventeenth century, German astronomer Johannes Kepler believed volcanoes were ducts for the earth's tears. I had eaten the last of my avocado, the ants marched onward with their wavering loads, and Arenal and I sat together and wept.

In my palm, all I had left of my avocado was the impossibly smooth pit. Stroking the slippery seed with my thumb, I held the pit to my cheek, the answer to the question I'd been asking all day—walking past the men on the street, sitting alone on the narrow bed, sheltering from the downpour against the warm building, careening toward the volcano on the jolting bus, taking in my first view of Arenal, my first volcano, and the ants, always leaving. I touched my lips to the unbroken shell, remembering how my mom had once used toothpicks to suspend an avocado pit over water in a jar, how amazed we were by the roots bursting through the casing, fissuring the pit like an eruption, or an accident.

Breaking open, to begin again.

Our son's birth was difficult. Before I could go into labor naturally, I panicked, suddenly sure he would die if we didn't get him out, so I asked to be induced. If the midwife would puncture the amniotic sac and bring my baby's head down to knock on the cervical door, I would finish the job. I would use my power to get him born, alive and breathing.

In the sixteenth hour, after the kind of pain that made me sure I would die, split open and die, the midwife told me it was time. She guided my hands down and touched them to my son's head—thick, wet hair and round, solid skull. I walked my fingers down to his ears. His ears!

"Now push and pull him up onto your chest," she instructed.

The doctor had arrived. He said, "Push past the burn. Feel the burn and push through it."

I felt the searing burn, on fire but not really a pain now, just flame. I clasped my baby's head, his ears tucked into my palms, and in a flood of my body's power, every kind of power, I pushed him out and guided his slippery body with my own hands up onto my waiting chest and our side of this crazy, hot, shifting, heartbreaking, beautiful world.

THE BABY AND THE ALLIGATOR

We learn about the horror too early in the morning these days.

Standing in the kitchen waiting for the coffee water to boil, hearing only the muted roaring and thumping of the gas flames on the metal pot, I act against my better instincts and reach for my phone sitting on top of the silent kitchen radio. The screen is so still and black that when I move in to check the news, I see the pale reflection of my hand like something rising up out of a dark pool.

The house sleeps. I want a few minutes to write before my kids wake up, so I have to be quiet. The phone doesn't make any noise, not like our local public radio guy with his boisterous celebrity birthday greetings, his warnings on windy days to "tie down the dachshund!"

But no Stan this morning. Stan is an esophageal cancer survivor, and now that he can speak again without coughing and hiccupping, Stan is loud—even at low volumes. His voice is like the rooster's crow in our family, calling the kids down to breakfast, and so I choose the phone instead, holding my thumb in the indentation to alert Siri and her circuit-board friends to my presence: I'm here, it's me, tell me what's going on. At my touch she comes to life, lighting up with a menu of colorful buttons, a handheld portal to everything I've missed in the night.

The world is reeling from the massacre in Orlando two nights before: forty-nine people killed in cold blood as they danced on

Latin night at Pulse, a gay nightclub named in honor of a brother fallen to AIDS—the sound of his heartbeat. I've been reading the stories of the victims: the couple whose families will honor their love by planning a joint funeral instead of a wedding, the Hoosier with the colorful bow ties who was always ready to help, the top-hat-wearing entrepreneur who ran a gay cruise line, the joyful young man who worked on the Harry Potter ride at Universal Studios and made J. K. Rowling cry at the unbearable news of his slaughter.

In audio released after the Orlando shooting—I can't listen—twenty-four rounds fire from the shooter's legally purchased MCX in nine seconds. The victims at Pulse were all together on one night, the body count staggering, the knowledge of what hate can do making me sick to my stomach, and I know we lose more people than that to guns every day in this country. We can't even pay attention to each loss, each family on its knees, rocking in keens of grief. The news becomes a smear of blood. A spill. The horror is so huge. Unthinkably, unimaginably huge.

So we don't think. We can't imagine. Our thoughts are with the families, we say. Our prayers are with the victims.

But maybe the victims don't want our thoughts and prayers.

They want something else. They want to open their eyes to a different world on a different day. They want their brothers husbands fathers sons sisters wives mothers daughters lovers friends to *not be dead*. They want to not have been shot. They want full use of their hands and brains and spines. And hearts.

I am thinking about guns. I am thinking about children. Under my bare feet, the tile feels cool, the glass on the phone silky smooth when I touch the fat white bird with the pad of my finger. I am so tired. *That bird is framed in blue*, I think. Tweet tweet.

NPR ✔ @NPR · Jun 15, 2016   ···
"Everyone at the Walt Disney World Resort is devastated by this tragic accident," Disney spokeswoman Jacquee Wahler said early Wednesday.

💬 6   ↻ 15   ♡ 35   ⬆️

NPR ✔ @NPR · Jun 15, 2016   ···
Replying to @NPR
A lifeguard on duty was unable to help, possibly because he was too far away.

💬 4   ↻ 4   ♡ 9   ⬆️

NPR ✔ @NPR · Jun 15, 2016   ···
Replying to @NPR
"The father did his best — he tried to rescue the child, however, to no avail," the spokesman said.

💬 2   ↻ 12   ♡ 14   ⬆️

Orlando again? A child? A lifeguard and a father? None of this makes any sense. I haven't even had my coffee. The silver kettle begins to scream—*No! Shhhhh!*—and I flip the phone onto the counter, face down. I don't want to look. I don't want to know. I reach for the handle, forgetting the pot holder and picking it up anyway, too hot on my palm, pouring the water over the grounds in the French press and watching them bubble up, black and steaming, a swamp.

I can't help it now. I have to keep reading, so I turn the phone over again, slide my finger up, scroll down, and get the news backward. First, the end—"Everyone at Walt Disney World is devastated by this tragic accident"—and then the beginning:

NPR ✔ @NPR · Jun 15, 2016   ···
Replying to @NPR
Sheriff's spokesman said the boy was playing at the edge of the water when the alligator attacked.

💬 3   ↻ 13   ♡ 3   ⬆️

NPR ✔ @NPR · Jun 15, 2016   ···
Replying to @NPR
The search -- which at one point overnight involved 50 people, two boats and an alligator tracker -- continues on Wednesday.

💬 4   ↻ 12   ♡ 11   ⬆️

NPR ✔ @NPR · Jun 15, 2016   ···
Alligator Grabs 2-Year-Old Near Disney's Grand Floridian Resort

This is today's news? An alligator stole a baby? Please no.

Here are the details on that first morning: A two-year-old boy was splashing ankle-deep in the water of the Seven Seas Lagoon at the Grand Floridian resort around nine in the evening. When the alligator snatched the boy, both parents were right there, and while the mother screamed for help, the father jumped in the lake to save their son. He wrestled the alligator.

The family was from Nebraska, vacationing at Disney World, cooling their heels by the manmade lake on the sugary sands near their resort—and an alligator rose up out of the dark water and made a jaw-snapping grab for the splashing boy. The stuff of nightmares. A nightmare these parents will have every night and every day for the rest of their heartbroken lives.

Later on this same day, I will find myself in the otherworldly setting of a dance recital dress rehearsal, sitting in the dark auditorium with the other mothers after my twelve-year-old's hair is pinned, her lipstick blotted. My girl, my firstborn, is on the stage in a sparkling crimson dress, angelic, but I'm feeling distracted, discombobulated. At this point, the toddler is still missing. The news is reporting an aggressive search-and-rescue operation, alligator trackers and trappers on the job, divers down deep, the magical world of Disney awash in the sickening throb of spinning emergency lights.

Sometimes we are simply in the wrong place at the wrong time, I think.

I wonder where they've taken the family to wait.

"Oh my God," I will say quietly, out of nowhere, out of the dark, between songs as the dance teacher offers critique to a circle of fairy-like girls in a pool of stage light, "that poor dad. I just keep thinking about the dad trying to save his baby from the alligator."

And my friend—a devoted, loving mother—will nod and say: "Well, there were warning signs about the alligators. The beach was posted 'no swimming.'"

I'm stunned when I hear this, but throughout the days and weeks that follow, until people stop talking about the baby and the alligator altogether, I will hear my friend's judgment echoed again and again and again. There were signs. Couldn't they read the signs? Those feckless parents got what they had coming.

The family was from Nebraska. I'm pretty sure there aren't a lot of alligators in Nebraska, and in fact, the signs said nothing about alligators lurking in the lake water kissing the immaculate, manicured white sand beaches of the resort, the very sands where Disney hosts family movie nights and fireworks. Signs about alligators would have been scary. So the signs didn't say: *Warning! Alligators. No Swimming.* The signs said simply: *No Swimming.*

Plus, the boy wasn't swimming. He was wading. He *couldn't* swim. He was only two.

Okay. But what if the signs *had* mentioned the alligators? Even so. Still.

My friend and I sit shoulder to shoulder in the dark. I don't know what to say, so I say what I'm feeling. "I don't care what the signs said. Those parents watched an alligator take their baby. It's just so sad."

I get that it feels better to imagine that all the bad things happen for a reason, and we are as individuals too smart/rich/wily/modest/white/straight/church-going/sign-reading to get shot or raped or robbed or seized by a wild animal and eaten/crushed/drowned. Empathy is the antidote to judgment, but we are a people who love to point fingers and draw boxes. *That* terrible thing? That will happen over there, to someone else, to someone who didn't follow the rules.

Me? On this side of the line? Safe, smart, smug. You? Over there? You're fucked. There were signs, and while the signs didn't say, "These waters are teeming with alligators that will snatch your happy, splashing toddler from the shallows and roll him under the water until he drowns," they did say: *No Swimming.*

So obviously these were bad parents who deserved to have their baby grabbed by an alligator.

Of course, when we can't feel someone else's pain, we can't really feel our own, either.

Also, there are so many rules. How could we ever follow them all?

In the kitchen, when I first touch my finger to my phone and read the news of the baby and the alligator, I am standing in front of the stove where I once set my skirt on fire when I (distractedly, ill-advisedly) used a dish towel instead of a pot holder to grab a boiling pasta pot off a high flame. We all make mistakes.

I don't have a lot of information about that horrible moment when the alligator rose up and bit down, but I can't stop my mind from going there. I know it was evening, so the family would already have had dinner—maybe the boy had eaten a couple of his chicken nuggets and an applesauce cup before crayoning his paper menu, maybe he was practicing making his letters, maybe he and his big sister got ice cream—but Nebraska's a time zone over from Florida, so it's likely the kids were still wide awake even though it was their normal bedtime. The parents figured a walk on the beach in front of the resort, some playtime, would help them get to sleep in the hotel room. When the baby splashed into the water, they might have pulled him back onto the sand at first, not wanting to deal with him getting his shorts wet, knowing there was a *No Swimming* sign, but then they might have figured, *What the heck? He's having so much fun. Let him tire himself out. He's about to change to pajamas anyway.*

Toes in the sand. Splashing. The whole family right there with the boy when the alligator did exactly what alligators have been doing for over thirty million years.

Maybe now, later, I could research the facts and learn more— how the family saved up for this vacation, what the parents did for work, which Disney ride the baby loved the best. I'm sure these are knowable things that became the stuff of public consumption in the weeks after the attack, but all of that feels private, and none of it matters to what consumes me. I remember that these suffering parents in the news are people, human beings like the rest of us, who love our children beyond measure.

So on that night in the magical kingdom, a tiny boy did what tiny boys do near water, and the alligator did what alligators do when small animals splash. And the father did what no father should ever have to do when the alligator's jaws snapped down. He threw himself onto the alligator and fought for his baby. There would have been no time for thinking or strategy. One moment, they were a family with their toes in the water of a manicured, white sand beach—it must have seemed so *safe*; everything about that family vacation moment was engineered to feel safe and happy—and the next, a lurking monster that had been only unseen eyeballs breaking the surface of the lake with barely a ripple, shining periscopes of reptilian vision, unleashed its coiled power, rising up out of the water with a tremendous splash and snap. There would have been no time to process a cogent thought, such as: *An alligator has my baby.* Only: *I need to get him back.* The alligator jumped on the boy, and the father jumped on the alligator, and when the alligator writhed and scraped free of the father's hands, sliding back into the deep, its jaws were still closed, the boy clamped in its immovable teeth.

Here, my imagination hits a black wall. The father's horror in this moment is beyond my power to envision. I grab the edge of the counter, something to hold onto while the room spins.

An alligator stole a baby. No more news.

I reach for the round knob on the coffee press, feeling the soft pressure in my palm and counting slowly to twenty as I plunge the filter through the thick grounds until I can push no farther. I pour the black coffee into my favorite mug and add a splash of half-and-half, stirring with a spoon, breathing, living my life, my daily life. Because I still can. Because yesterday I was in the right places at the right times and everyone I loved was too. Because when it's not your tragedy, you can feel your empathy, your true sorrow, and then you can let it go. You can let the horror sink back to wherever it came from and go back to drinking your coffee, tweeting your tweets, living your life.

Days pass and the news keeps coming, uncoiling, rising up.

The search for the baby ended after sixteen hours. Divers found the boy's body six feet below the surface, just over ten feet from where the alligator pulled him under. Somehow this seems too close. In the photo released by his family, the boy is smiling, beautiful blue eyes shining, and his snazzy zipper-neck sweater makes him look older than two but for the pudge on the back of his sweet hand.

A few days after the alligator attack, I read more news: a mother in Colorado heard a scream coming from the backyard where her two boys were playing and ran outside to see a mountain lion hunched over her five-year-old. She did what the father had done with the alligator, with the same speed, the same adrenaline-fired strength that comes from loving someone so much you don't think before dying for them. The boy's mother jumped onto the lion's back, and like a wrestler preparing to pin, she pulled back the paws and found her son's whole head in the lion's mouth. She grabbed the jaws, top and bottom, and wrenched them open. An alligator bites down with seven times the force of a mountain lion. Like the alligator, this lion was young and relatively small. The lion lost its grip. The mother got her boy back alive.

When I read this story, I am amazed, of course, relieved to know the mother won, but my next thought is: *I hope the father who lost his boy is not hearing this news today.*

My daughter, Ella, is fascinated by politics and current events. Tonight she has been reading a weekly news magazine, and we find ourselves in the tiny bathroom at the same time. In the quiet and solitude, she leans against me, looking mournful. "Do you think it's just me or do you think the world is really going downhill?" She makes a motion with her fine-boned hand, a dancer's hand, sled-like, slipping down a mountain of air in our bathroom. Downhill.

"Oh, honey," I say. "I know. It's been an awful week."

"I didn't want to say anything with Henry around," she begins, "but there was *another* shooting in Orlando, too. A singer." Henry is her little brother. She wants to shield him from fear and sorrow.

I nod and then shake my head. Christina Grimmie. I don't know what to say except, "Yes, I know." I'm holding her against my chest, my chin on the back of her head, my arms wrapped around her thin body. I see her face in the mirror and feel the tears now, splashing onto my hands.

She looks up and catches my eyes in the mirror. "People keep *killing* other people, Mom. It's just so . . ." She pauses. "It's just so *sad*."

In the wake of the most horrible news, I sometimes remind my kids of what Mr. Rogers said after something terrible happened: "When I was a boy and I would see scary things in the news, my mother would say to me, 'Look for the helpers. You will always find people who are helping.'" There are so many good people, I tell them.

After Christina Grimmie was shot three times, her brother tackled the shooter, the shooter somehow shot himself in the ensuing struggle—and that was the end of it. There were more than a hundred people around the merchandise table when the killer approached, hugged Grimmie, and then fired his first three shots into her body at close range, at hug range. Grimmie's brother has been hailed as a hero for all the lives he likely saved, but Grimmie died of her wounds. Her brother is a hero who lost the one he needed most to save.

My daughter is right. The news this week does not stop coming.

I read that Brenda Lee Marquez McCool, a single mother of eleven, was "like the mom of Pulse." She danced the salsa, tearing up the floor, and she was there dancing with her son Isaiah on the night of the attack. When the shooter aimed his gun in their direction, she screamed at Isaiah to "get down!" and standing between that ugly gun and her beautiful son, she took two bullets. She died protecting her son. I've seen a photo of McCool posted on Facebook—cropped blond hair, dangling earrings, black spaghetti straps—and the look in her dark eyes is so steady. So focused.

Sometimes I wonder how much news I can hear, and more, whether we should censor the magazines and newspapers our daughter reads with such care and focus and broken-hearted tears—but then I remember that turning away and shutting down cannot be the answer for any of us. Ella's weeping is the appropriate response to a devastating week. I once read that the core of the struggle for our children is that they see what a mess the world is, and they don't always feel confident that the adults who are supposedly in charge possess the necessary competence to fix things. This makes sense.

We need to get a grip. Enacting the kind of political and social change we need to address gun violence, racism, poverty, prejudice, violence, and brutality of every form and magnitude may begin with just the kind of pain Ella is feeling. It *hurts* to think about how afraid the Pulse victims were when they were locked in with the shooter in that bathroom or how it felt to be a father waiting outside the hospital to find out if his son had been brought in, if he was still breathing. It's supposed to hurt.

As I get older, with so much more to lose, I struggle to bring my mind to those places where I can't help but pray my life will never take me. Sometimes the wall at the border of empathy feels like a physical barrier in my mind, a metal plate clanging down to stop the firing of synapses, the mirror neurons lighting up like emergency vehicles at the scene of an accident.

It's too much. Better to get away, go somewhere, anywhere, else: a social media rabbit hole, a workout, the grocery store.

Even writing this story, I want to type the words *unimaginable, unthinkable, unspeakable*—and stop. Is it unimaginable? If you were in that bathroom? Or waiting outside that hospital? Or on your knees in the still-churning water with nothing to hold in your hands but sand?

Are we born feeling the pain of others, or is empathy something we have to learn and practice? Science tells us that—as with so many things—it's a little of both, and children who are getting their own emotional needs met are better positioned to give empathy freely. Ella is a born empath. She's like a child from a fairy tale who treads down the forest path in bare feet with her little heart light glowing. All the creatures come out to greet her because they know she would never harm them. For example, she is the only person I know who employs a catch-and-release method for trapping mosquitoes that get into our house. She uses a cup and a sheet of paper to return them to the outdoors.

When Ella was in first grade, we too took a family vacation to Florida. We were out on a warm and breezy afternoon, happy, exploring the town, when we rounded a corner and came face to face with a charred turning body, a little pig roasting on a spit. The pig was stretched, bound by blackening ankles over a smoldering pit. Ella screamed, whirled around, and used her own body to block her three-year-old brother's sightline. "Don't look, little buddy," she cried. "Don't look!"

Afterward, around the corner from the poor pig, down on the curb, holding her head in her hands, she moaned, betrayed by the world, betrayed by *me*, and said with conviction: "I am *never* going to eat anything that was alive again." Her round cheeks were streaked with tears, but her blue eyes were fierce. "Never."

Since that afternoon, she hasn't eaten a morsel of meat.

The whole world happens to Ella. Life won't be easy for her.

There are more good people than bad people, I tell my kids, because I believe that. In this one week, we were reminded that we live in a world where fathers and mothers and brothers will fight monsters—an alligator, a lion, a spray of bullets, a madman. Here is love we can see, love we can look at and understand, even as the sheer magnitude of terror threatens to occlude our vision with a sorrow so big we have to struggle to hold it all.

The baby's father leapt onto that alligator, grabbing for anything he could hold—rough skin, sharp claws, tight jaws. He fought for a grip, a release, for the dear life of his boy. Also: the mother with her hands in the lion's mouth, the brother throwing himself between his already bleeding sister and the gun that killed her. All such violent, horrible images—hearts that break, hearts forever broken but staggering in the force of their love.

Here is something I have learned from this week's news. Here is what I will keep. If we could reach back in time and give Brenda McCool the power of breath, she would stand in the same position, in love, between her son and those bullets: again and again and again.

AISKHYNE

The semester had worn me down. I was chairing too many com-
mittees, attending too many meetings, writing too many emails,
and right then, I was grading essays in my lap as I inched toward
the window for the Grande Flat White I needed like a shot of
adrenaline to my faltering heart to keep on keeping on. Under
the mermaid, on the side of the brick building, the big letters
reminded me I was in the *Drive-thru*. Why not *through*? What's
the marketing goal in the casual spelling? We want the easy thing,
the fast thing. Are we texting here or making a sign that's going
to be on a wall for *years*? I made a mental circle on the brick wall
with my purple pen, raised my foot from the brake, and slipped
forward another car length.

The previous week, our twelve-year-old daughter, Ella, had been
diagnosed with a fast-progressing scoliosis that had curved her
spine into a question mark, and now the specter of a spinal fusion
surgery was a black cloud slipping toward us like a low-bellied cat.
Keeping one eye on the cloud took all my strength. I was numb,
tired, unfocused. Circling *parent's* in *my parent's basement* (and
scribbling *weren't there 2?*) for the tenth time that day, I considered
the dumb ease with which I'd just ordered a $5 *medium* coffee
with an Italian word that actually means "large," thinking, *They
finally got me*, just as the suits in their marketing and branding
meetings lo those many years ago had projected they would. *The
public can be trained*, someone must have said—and so we can.

I put down the essays to get out my wallet, and when my fingers
touched the cool, smooth glass of my phone, I pulled that out,

too, because . . . because *phone*. Because *shiny*. Because I felt like shit, and the sleek device in my hand lit up like a personal slot machine in the dark casino of my sad head. Maybe something good had happened. Maybe I'd won something. Maybe somebody liked me. Tired and low, it didn't occur to me to think, *Nothing good and lasting comes from a push or a number or a notification. I will not, in this phone, find a cure for scoliosis. I will not pull up a magic wand to wave over her spine, mumble an incantation, and watch the question mark straighten into an affirmative exclamation point that will keep her dancing.*

On Twitter, Southwest Airlines had popped into my feed to tell me they were running a contest to win free flights. Quick: your most embarrassing moment in 140 characters or fewer. #wannagetaway #contest

I started to run worthy embarrassing moments in my mind—there were quite a few back there to choose from—and before I'd rolled up for my turn at the window, I had already remembered, and dismissed, that time in my early twenties when, staying the night with a new boyfriend I had been led to believe lived alone, I'd sashayed down to the kitchen wearing nary a stitch to check the pizza in the hot oven (a bad idea on multiple levels). I was bent over, head in the oven, fanny up, when a dude I'd never seen before—who *lived there*—appeared in the doorway. I screamed, he screamed, we all screamed. Embarrassing, but how to explain in 140 characters the lack of communication between me and this boyfriend who eventually revealed himself to be a giant fink? Too complicated.

I paid for the coffee, clenching the green spill stopper in my teeth, and hurried home to finish grading before it was time to pick up the kids.

When I got home, I did not grade. The first one I typed up was easy:

Student: Professor Christman? I don't know how to tell you this.
Me: What?
Student: Umm. Your skirt is falling off.
#wannagetaway #contest

True story, but hard—in 140 characters—to express how far the skirt had fallen (below the level of my pubis, but the gods of modesty had given me tights to wear that day) and how much pleasure this particular student had gleaned from what appeared on the surface to be an act of bold mercy. Still. Not bad. *Your skirt is falling off.*

But since Southwest said I could enter as many times as I wanted and those essays were still waiting to be graded, I started another, but it grew to four parts—what I consider a Twitter cheat—and in the final turn, I was hit by a surprise:

> #wannagetaway #contest It's 1980 & I'm 11, bespectacled & chubby: invited (finally!) to a sleepover with the Izod- & Nike-wearing girls.

> Pick-up time & my mom rings the doorbell in dirty gardening overalls & a blue bandanna. Behind her, our Chevy truck, duct-taped together.

> Girls crowd around the door in one unit, like puppies, to see this strange, dirty mother. *They're poor*, I hear. I burn with embarrassment.

> Now I am the mother, & I think of mine, stopping her digging to pick me up, dirt smudged & smiling, so happy to see me after my night away.

In Greek, there are two different words meaning shame.
Aidos is modesty: it's what I was feeling when I pulled my head out of the oven, face flaming, or yanked up my skirt.

Aiskhyne is what I feel now: I am disgraced. I flush with a shame that feels like fever. My mother left her digging to come get me, her ungrateful daughter. I was embarrassed by her overalls and her dirty bandanna, and I told her so. As a child, I witnessed my mother behaving in many different ways—she was consistently generous and hardworking, and she could be irresponsible, playful, or even high as a kite—but I never, ever, not even once, saw her be mean to anyone.

Where did I get it, my meanness? Was I born that way? Did I learn it from the other girls?

Before this moment, this *second*, I'd never revisited this incident with anything more thoughtful than laughter. I remember the scene through a beautifully draped window, my mother pulling her truck into the frame of our slumber-party vision and me knowing there was no way to hide: the rumbling old green truck with all the rust covered over with duct tape so it could pass inspection, the paint-splattered overalls my mom wore at her second (or third) job renovating houses, the bandanna she tied on to keep her curls off her face when she worked.

Even into adulthood, I had hung onto the narrative as something that was done to *me*, that my mother had somehow set me up for judgment, as if I were a mere pair of muddy overalls and a blue headscarf away from being embraced by these girls with their canopy beds, wall-to-wall carpeting, and vast collections of Strawberry Shortcake dolls. I was not that much younger than my own daughter is now when I heard the whispers at that door—*They're poor*—and carried the shame those mean girls handed to me right down the walkway and into the dusty green truck, where I glowered at my mother, crying angry tears and feeling forsaken by *her*, not the pink-cheeked devils who peeked out from behind the curtains.

Now? I own overalls. I get dirty in our garden. I'm not much of a kerchief wearer, but I certainly make it through many weekend days without running a brush through my hair. There must be times when Ella feels embarrassed by me—or at least *for* me.

But if she does, she never shows it. I've never seen or heard Ella being mean.

Every morning before school, Ella pats baby powder on her body from armpits to waist, pulls a tank top on to protect her broken skin, and then she brings me her back brace—it's molded plastic and foam with wide Velcro straps, a Boston brace. She wriggles into place and then turns her back to me so I can pull those straps with all my might, knee against her body, securing her brace with the same force I'd use to tighten the cinch on a saddle. The idea is to pull the spine back into alignment. The brace hurts, but Ella follows the ortho's instructions, wearing the brace for at least twenty hours each day. When she takes it off in the evening to bathe, her flesh looks like a wood block print, the hard lines of the brace painted over the white curves of her belly and back. I help her smooth on cream to quiet the rash, she applies the powder, and then sucks in her breath as I pull the straps into place for the night. "You can go tighter, Mom," she says. "It's okay. I'm okay." She wants the brace to do its work, to make it so she doesn't need the surgery after all. She forgives me every time.

Today, I want to take a lesson from my daughter's grace and apologize for real.

Mom, I'm so sorry I took the hurt those girls handed me at the door that day and tried to give it to you. Also? I think you look adorable in overalls, and I'm grateful to you for teaching me how to nurture living things, even if you insist that I'm the one with the green thumb. You were right. A marigold, tipping its yellow face to the sun, will grow pretty much anywhere. I think of you every spring when I slip the roots from the box and tuck each happy flower into the clay by my front stoop. Thank you for your lessons in color and kindness.

THE LUCKY ONES

I carry fears around the way some women accumulate old lipsticks in the bottom of their handbags. In fact, I'm one of those women, too. Most days, this works out okay, but sometimes I leave my bag in a hot car or the sharp end of one of my keys knocks the lid off a tube—who knows how it happens, really?—and then the next time I reach into the depths of my bag for a fallen tin of mints or the magnetic sunglasses that are forever eluding me, I feel something wet, something gooey, and my hand comes back up looking as if I've been in some kind of accident, like instead of being the kind of woman who lets old lipsticks accumulate, I might be another kind, the kind who keeps razor blades in the bottom of her bag, just in case. That's how gruesome melted Sheer Ambrosia Fire looks under the nails and between the fingers. Like some kind of warning.

Of course, I intend to clean the lipsticks out, and on these bad days, I do, because I have no other choice. I lay out a sheet of newspaper on the dining room table and I shake the bag upside down, letting the detritus of my quotidian life rain or float down, depending on weight and density. Back in grad school, when I was a smoker, there was always a dusting of tobacco and the clank of a dead lighter or two, sometimes the lepidopteran flap of the spare flights I carried—for real—for late-night darts at the bar. But that, as I'm trying to get to here, was a long, long time ago, and while today's dusty bits are usually the crumbs of granola bars or a crushed Tylenol, I know I should be a better person by now.

I should have made more progress, and I shouldn't be so afraid. I should be a person who has her act together, inside and out. I should be a person who has designated *compartments* in her purse—one for a phone, one for a wallet, one for those blasted sunglasses, and one with a zipper for the lipsticks: just two at a time, a tinted lip balm and a color. Have you seen these women in the department stores or, most astoundingly, at the ticket counter in the airport with their coordinated luggage? How they unsnap their handbags, reach in with manicured fingers, and pull back just the thing you imagine those enviable fingers reached in to retrieve? How *smooth* they make this reaching seem, as if their whole lives are this effortless, this finding of things without even looking. And what is that smell rising up from this immaculate place? Fresh leather, like a new car, with mint and floral notes at the finish.

In my bag? Pens. So many pens. A murder of pens, a collision of pens. Maybe I need two pens—black and blue. Not eight, not twelve. That's too many pens. How can I possibly write with them all every day? How does the purple pen, the playful shade I turn to most often for commenting on student essays, feel when she sifts down to the bottom of the pile and I forget her there?

On the days when something so bad happens in my purse that I can no longer pretend I'm coping, I try to choose the sports page or the classifieds for the dumping, but I should probably try to find something with no words at all. Next time, I should cut open a brown paper bag and use the blank inside, because I'm distracted by all those words peeping out from beneath the lipsticks, pens, Post-its, receipts, hair clips, and plastic junk from the dentist that the children greedily collect but never think about again: royal family finger puppets, rubber bracelets promoting flossing, weird gooey things in shapes of tree frogs or human hands that adhere when you fling them at windows. Imagine one of those sticky, stretchy hands, a translucent red, after a month at the bottom of my purse, dusted with crumbs and stray hairs, reaching with clotted jelly fingers to touch the word *clean*.

Such aspiration from a misfit toy! My dumped purse and the newsprint are a mixed-media found poem, but right now I need to focus. I am trying to find the center of a metaphor: *lipsticks are to the bottom of the handbag as fears are to the amygdala.* I am no kind of brain scientist, but I used to work in a cognitive psychology lab; fundamentally, the amygdala is responsible for implicit memory—emotional responses connected to fear. I want to shake out the implicit from where it lies curled in the amygdala, loosen this tight knot of hidden fears, spread the images across the paper, and then maybe find a place to store them in the hippocampus with the explicit memories, with the memories I can at least pretend to understand.

The truth? I worry too much.

I worry about a lot of things, but mostly, I worry about the physical safety of my kids. All the time. To be fair to myself—I try—we've been through a year of orthopedic trials. Last November, our son fell twenty feet out of a tree, fracturing his pelvis, and our daughter was diagnosed with scoliosis severe enough to require spinal fusion surgery. The surgery was last month. Risks included infection, paralysis, blindness, bleeding, death. After the surgeon's shot of morphine in her spinal cord wore off, she endured a few days of brutal pain, but holding a cold cloth to her forehead and a warm one to her belly, I'd think, *You're alive, you're alive, thank God you're alive.* As I said, it was a year. Somewhere in the open pockets of my brain I can almost see a tiny version of myself crawling among the spare buttons and threads of memory, and I can tell you, she looks frazzled. Her nerves are shot.

Off crutches now, my son scowls as he heads for the nearest tree, daring me to warn him down: he is not afraid, and he doesn't want me to stop him from doing "anything that's at all fun forever." My daughter, still recovering, brushes me away when I arrive with a footstool or another pillow to ease the pressure on her back. "Mom. Seriously. I'm fine."

My worry isn't good for them—and it isn't good for *me*.

I was sexually abused as a child. I have written the story of those years again and again, in fiction and nonfiction, from far away and from right up close. Repeatedly diagnosed with post-traumatic stress disorder, I have lots of practice *remembering* the traumatic events (at least some of them) without *reliving* the traumatic events. Also, there was the car accident that killed my fiancé when I was twenty. I wasn't there, but for years, even though I didn't hear the wailing that arrived at the devastating scene to pronounce him dead, the sirens, any sirens, were like an oyster knife in my heart.

But I'm wondering if my worry problem is not these huge brain-changers but the accumulation of smaller dangers, the accretion of minor fears on the shores of my brain, the flotsam and jetsam—the kind that make us laugh, the kind that to the casual, outside observer seem like quirks of my personality. I won't go so far as to hope anyone finds them charming, but like the rattling lipstick tubes in the bottom of my purse, they aren't really hurting anyone.

Are they?

Exempli gratia: I am terrified of projection screens. Specifically, I am afraid one will fall on my face when I'm either pulling it down or pulling it up.

I have seen it happen.

Because I am a teacher, this fear of projection screens and the possibility that the heavy metal casing will slip from its anchors and smash my face does, in fact, affect my daily life. I teach essay-writing, so airing my terror about falling screens to my students actually has a defensible pedagogical underpinning. I am *modeling* the process of essaying. Here is this thing that waits for me at the back of my brain that no one else can see: What do I do with it? Where are the patterns and connections? How do we make meaning? Where do things fall apart? Plus, my example isn't scary or triggering for any of my students. Who's afraid of a projector screen? As their artsy, oddball teacher, I am comic, not tragic.

But. When I reach for the dangling string to engage the roller mechanism on the screen and pull it down into an extended and locked position, a tabula rasa on which we can project our work of the day, a thunderbolt of adrenaline rocks my body.

One moment, I am a professor wearing teacher black and well-heeled boots, clicking around at the front of the classroom as if I have every right and reason in the world to be there. Then my fingers curl around the cord to pull downward, meet the resistance of the mechanism—I'm trying to pull down, but *it* wants to coil up—and I feel a jolt of fear right in my heart, a shock of sweat to my armpits and forehead. The tiny hairs on the back of my neck vibrate, sending out distress signals, and my tongue, sucked of moisture, tastes as if I have just eaten a teaspoon of instant coffee, bitter and dry. I cannot swallow.

Sometimes I can fight through this moment, breathing in through my nose and out through my mouth, coaxing the screen down into a locked position, but if the screen gets stuck or sucks back into its casing or makes any kind of unusual noise, I can't do it. I step back, hands up in a gesture of surrender, and ask for a brave volunteer: "Hannah, would you get this for me?"

Usually we're far enough into the semester that the students know the story. Most are sympathetic. It's hard to be human, isn't it? We accumulate so much over the years. Sometimes there's more than we can carry alone.

Here is the long version of the story I tell my students:

When I was in fourth grade I attended an elementary school in Newbury, Massachusetts, we all called "the Round School"— although, in truth, the school was shaped like a lollipop, and the kindergarten and the third and fourth grades were housed in the stick. At the Round School, I had a young, pretty teacher whom I adored: Mrs. Daniels. She had short dark hair, and while I wore owl glasses and loomed like a fairy-tale giant over all the other boys and girls in my class, I got my hair done in a pixie cut so I would match Mrs. Daniels. By the end of the year, Mrs. Daniels was heavily pregnant, and while I certainly knew the condition of pregnancy meant she was going to have a baby, I don't remember truly understanding either the details or the ramifications. It didn't matter. She was my teacher and I loved her. What's a swallowed pumpkin between two smart girls with pixie cuts who love to read?

And then one day, there was an accident—right at the front of our classroom, right before our very eyes. It was spring, and the windows were cranked open. Mrs. Daniels walked to the center of the room, reached up, grabbed the cord to pull down the screen for the overhead projector—and the whole, big, metal, hulking thing slipped from the brackets on the wall and crashed onto her upturned face.

There was blood. That's all I really remember. Mrs. Daniels was on the floor on her knees, holding her face in her hands. Blood gushed from between her fingers and splashed onto the spread of fabric covering her round belly. The wide canvas of her maternity dress—I can't remember the color, but it was tent-like and pastel—displayed the expanding blossoms of deep-red blood to a gruesome effect. I realize now that what was happening then and what happened after had nothing to do with the condition of pregnancy and everything to do with physics and the heavy momentum of a screen falling from its brackets and being caught by Mrs. Daniels's *face*, but in my young mind, somehow, what we kids were witnessing *was* pregnancy or birth or something, and it was terrifying. Bloody and impossible.

How did all the other grown-ups get into the room? Did Mrs. Daniels call for them or were nearby teachers alerted by the sound of the crash? The story my hippocampus has made of the scene has no audio track, only images, and I can't see the other kids in the memory either. Only Mrs. Daniels, her face occluded by her spread and bloody fingers—and then the other grown-ups. No kids move around the periphery of this memory. We are a locked frame of fear. I can feel the smooth, molded desk chair under my legs as if it is a part of my body, the ridge mid-thigh, as if I will never go anywhere without that chair again.

So much blood.

Who were all those grown-ups? The principal? Other teachers? The school nurse? At some point, the grown-ups helped Mrs. Daniels up off the ground, led her away, and memory stops.

That's it. My brain failed to record the ending, and maybe that's why I'm doomed to keep replaying the narrative, a pop-song earworm for which I don't know the lyrics. Here's the thing: Mrs. Daniels never came back. The screen fell, Mrs. Daniels fell, the blood flowed from her face and onto her belly like the first plague of Egypt upon the earth—and then they led her away. The next morning, a substitute was sitting at her desk when we came in, we were told nothing I can remember about our missing teacher, and the final days of the school year turned to summer without her return.

I can't remember ever seeing Mrs. Daniels again, and somewhere along the way into the various compartments of my brain, the details jumble and conflate: Mrs. Daniels and falling screens and gushing blood and late pregnancy and the way in which someone we love can be there one minute and gone the next—forever.

While the grown-up me recognizes that all of that blood must have been coming from her nose or even a cut in her forehead—as a mother I've learned that noses and head wounds bleed a *lot*— the menace of the overhead projector screen has stayed with me, adhered in a complicated way to the mystery and danger of pregnancy and stuck altogether to something that feels like . . . what? Abandonment. My brain would have me believe that Mrs. Daniels never even came back to say good-bye, and maybe it's that betrayal that gave me this fear to carry all these years, through the mysteries of sex and adolescence, well into adulthood, and onward into my own turn to don a maternity dress and float around the front of a classroom in the long shadow of the overhead projector screen. We were pixie-cut twins who loved words, and she left without ever saying good-bye.

Was she *dead*? Did she *die*? Did the baby *die*?

Surely not.

Surely not. Right?

Surely my fear is out of proportion with the actual risk of falling overhead projector screens. Statistically speaking, I should be more afraid of slipping in someone's spilled latte or taking a sharpened pencil to the eyeball. There's a logical explanation for Mrs. Daniels's disappearance. We were nearing the end of the school year, and she was nearing delivery. It probably just made sense to start her maternity leave. I'm guessing it's as simple as that, and my nine-year-old mind made way too much of what I saw that afternoon when the screen came crashing down.

I don't have to let my brain kill her off when I can just as easily tell myself a different story. I can write a plausible ending in which Mrs. Daniels is *fine*. Her baby would now be nearly forty years old. He's likely very handsome with raven-colored hair and sparkling eyes. Perhaps he's working in set design on Broadway, divorced with two children of his own, and of course it's too bad about the marriage, but he's taken a new lover and everyone seems happier. And Mrs. Daniels, well, she's coming up on seventy, still spry, enjoying retirement, keeping the grandkids when she can and traveling—always with a notebook in her bag to record all the most delicious details. She still loves to read, but she never could make the transition to an e-reader, even though her son got her a Kindle for Christmas a few years back, so her suitcase is always heavy with too many books.

I wonder how she wears her hair.

Here's the main thing: the falling screen didn't kill her, and it didn't kill her baby. Brain, do you hear me? Mrs. Daniels is *fine*.

A few days ago, my thirteen-year-old daughter said something that chilled my heart. We were on a postprandial family walk. My husband was chasing after our nine-year-old son, who was careening down the street on his bicycle, having just swerved erratically from one side of the street—against traffic (although there was none), where he shouldn't have been riding—to the other, where an actual bicyclist was zipping along. Although the actual bicyclist shouldn't have been going so fast, I am grateful he was paying close attention; he swerved expertly, avoiding a direct collision with our son and swooping around the corner and out of sight like a bat into the dying light. A woman walking two Corgis paused to clutch her heart and say, "That was scary, wasn't it?" Indeed.

Afterward, with the menfolk zipping ahead, I was telling my daughter how I wasn't sure how our friends could bear to let their son just head out into the world on his bike on summer mornings and trust that he'd return in one piece at dinnertime. Even though that's how my entire generation lived our lives, back when there was nothing called "free-range parenting," and in fact "parent" wasn't even a verb. That's just what kids did in the summer while their parents were at work—they roamed on bikes, alone and in packs, peeling out in gravel lots, no hands, no helmets, plywood ramps on blocks in the middle of the road for Evil Knievel jumps. It was a banner safety awareness day when no one decided it would be a good idea to set the ramp on fire.

"Well," she said, "you *have* kept us on a pretty short leash."

"Do you want a longer leash?"

"It's too late," she said, shaking her head. "Everything seems scary."

Shit, I thought. I tried so hard to *not* do this to her. Now how do I *undo* it? And I know the answer to that question is: I don't. Now *she* has to undo it, but I can try to be better.

Philip Larkin comes to mind. *They fuck you up, your mum and dad . . .*

You know a major contributor to the mess of our brain bags these days? The internet. Here I've written myself to a perfectly good

159

conclusion, a remaking of the Mrs. Daniels story, one in which both she and her firstborn son are healthy and hale, and then I think, well, I suppose I should at least do a quick search, but I don't really want to because what if the news is bad? What if I uncover the tragic report of one Mrs. Daniels, fourth-grade teacher at Newbury Elementary, suffering a brain hemorrhage after a freak classroom accident? A death made even more tragic by the associated demise of her unborn child?

The true ending of this story matters to Mrs. Daniels herself—maybe. Then again, maybe it ceased to matter to her a long, long time ago. But does it really matter to my cluttered brain? Is the internet really going to help me clear my skull of the benign horrors clinging in the dusty corners, those quotidian fears that hold me back from grabbing onto the cord of that screen at the front of my classroom and giving it a good, firm yank? Is it going to help me loosen the leash my daughter feels too tightly wrapped around her?

Not hardly. The internet is a big pile of garbage through which we daily choose to wade. We rarely find what we're looking for in the pile, but does that stop us?

Never.

Within seconds I'm on the website of the Newbury Elementary School, which still seems to house the same grades—this surprises me because it has always struck me as strange that the first and second grades were farmed out to a different building in another part of town, but New Englanders are nothing if not bound by tradition. Of course, just because Mrs. Daniels is no longer listed on the faculty page, we shouldn't assume her to be long-dead, killed by an overhead projector screen in the bloom of her youth and fertility, as a consideration of the calendar alone tells us she would have been long-retired. What the blow of the screen may have spared, the mounting years will soon take anyway.

I ask my mother, but while the name "sounds familiar," she doesn't remember Mrs. Daniels or the accident; I don't even have a first name for my search, nothing to go on beyond *Newbury Elementary School teacher Daniels*. Following these desultory crumbs, I find a website devoted to the history of this coastal region of Massachusetts where residents write in to record their memories. Deep in the internet forest, hoping to stumble upon a Mrs. Daniels through serendipity alone, and bolstered by the idea that if I had loved her, others had as well, I keep clicking and reading. Shouldn't she be a feature in the town's collective memory?

Page leads on to page, and before long I find myself in a corner of the site titled "Murders, Suicides, Unfortunate Accidents." I don't even need to make this stuff up. If Mrs. Daniels had been *killed* by that projector screen, where else would I find a record of that event? I don't find Mrs. Daniels, but what I do find makes me grateful, not for the first time, that I made it out of childhood on that particular stretch of New England coast alive.

The page kicks off with a suicide: the butcher who killed himself in the back of his father's shop—with a gun. The contributor calls the butcher's choice of instrument "ironic." Do we expect all butchers to use meat cleavers for their last job? As kids, we went to Fowles to eat pancakes at the few booths behind the counter where the locals, fishermen and carpenters, sat for long hours drinking coffee and talking about winds, tides, and tools. This was the 1970s, the same decade as the butcher's suicide, and I wonder if I heard about the tragedy and forgot, not understanding, or if I ate bacon he had cut with his big knife, licking the salty grease from my fingers. The chances seem good.

After the butcher's story, the site moves into murders, and everyone has a lot to say about one young and beautiful Mrs. Clark, who stabbed *and* shot her husband, wrapped his body in electrician's wire, weighted it with cement blocks, and dumped him into the river. The unfortunate Mr. Clark, who in his better days had been an enthusiastic wife-swapper, was discovered a couple months later in a tangle of marsh grass by an unlucky birdwatcher. The crime was dubbed "The Palm Sunday Murder," and Mrs. Clark was convicted of second-degree murder and sentenced to fifty years. My favorite detail is not the suspicion that this twenty-something mother of three had an accomplice, likely a lover, who helped her to dump her 160-pound, wire-bound husband into the river, and whom she protected with her silence, but the damning evidence that the cement blocks used to weight the body had been pried from the foundation of their family home like broken teeth. I don't call that ironic, but it's certainly not the kind of metaphor you want girding your family story.

There are many more murders—the florist, the reporter's wife, the elderly woman who lived above the Fruit Basket, poor Karen on the bunny trail—but what gets me, of course, is the long list of "unfortunate accidents." No falling screens, no Mrs. Daniels, but Lordy, so much crushing, bleeding, electrocuting, drowning—everybody, all the time, drowning. Here is the place where I roamed free as a kid, riding my bike from the island to the mainland during low tide to have a cup of chili at the restaurant where my mother was a waitress, then back again across the Merrimac, the river that stars in so many of the unfortunates: stories of teenagers hitting their heads on docks and falling backward into the dark swirl, rowboats washing up empty on the beach, or the worst, a poor kid who jumped from the B&M railroad bridge and got entangled in a coil of cable. By the time the divers brought him up, they say the currents had stretched his body to ten feet long.

A man I don't know but who would have been my contemporary sums up our childhood: "Most of us had tempted fate to a greater or lesser degree during our youth. Dumb-ass games of bow and arrow or with a .22 rifle in an enclosed basement. Tunnels, ice-flows, water-towers. Overloaded boats with no flotation devices. Yeah, we were not the bright ones, but we were the lucky ones."

The jumbled bag of the brain works together, of course, but it's the hippocampus who's the well-thumbed Moleskine notebook in this picture, sorting out the details and working on the narrative of the accident: it was Mrs. Daniels, we were in fourth grade, she was pregnant, etcetera. The amygdala is the Nervous Nancy who brings the jolt to the heart, the sudden wash of sweat: Watch out! It's falling! Ever vigilant to triggers, she is the one who sounds the alarm, and in me, the amygdala is strong. She keeps her head on a swivel, and she never takes a break.

I should no longer be afraid of overhead projector screens. Despite my preference to avoid the chore, in my twenty-five years in the classroom I have pulled down screens hundreds, if not thousands, of times—and no screen has ever fallen on me. If there's anything at all to be said for reconditioning, my brain should have long ago replaced the fear response associated with the fourth-grade accident with the simple humdrum of daily life in a room with an overhead projector. The stimulus should be losing power. The metallic grind of the retraction mechanism should no longer send me under the desk with the surge protectors, dust bunnies, and dried-out highlighters—but it does.

Human brains are wired for rapid automatic responses. Fast action can save our lives. Say you're walking along a wooded path and you catch a glimpse of something coiled, black, and shiny out of the corner of your eye. You leap sideways, and then— safely on the other side of the path—you finish processing that flash of an image, recognize that the giant snake you just saw is actually a discarded loop of garden hose, and laugh at yourself. These side-jumping automatic responses are balanced by the responses we actually *plan* when we have a few seconds—or, say, a lifetime—to consider the details. Basically, the amygdala and the prefrontal cortex (including the hippocampus) work together to give humans the capacity to exercise control over the things that scare us, but this same capacity, when applied with extra diligence, allows us to imagine the failure of a given scenario or dangers that don't exist. In other words, we can think our way in and out of our own fear.

It's possible I suffer from an excess of imagination. Context is everything, and God is in the details. I live my life through the twin tenets of curiosity and close observation. I believe imagination and storytelling are central to our survival as a species—and yet, it's my imagination that makes me jumpy. A projector screen is not (that) scary, but as quickly as my prefrontal can remind my amygdala of this fact, my amygdala can counter with her *maybes* and *what ifs* and *yes, but perhaps this time the maintenance guy left the last screw in his pocket.*

I dump my brain bag out onto the spread newspaper and start sorting: things I need, things I don't need but can't bear to get rid of, things that are damaged beyond repair, and things I never should have saved in the first place. I do the work of necessary maintenance. We'll never chronicle all the things that might be piling up to get us—loose projector screens, doomed pregnancies, murderous jilted wives, coiled cable, rising tides. I mean, look at my own family in just this year—a fall from a tree and adolescent idiopathic scoliosis. A year ago today, I wasn't afraid of trees, and scoliosis was something that existed only vaguely in the bend-over tests they had us perform in middle-school PE. But now? They're on my list.

In the forty years since Mrs. Daniels's accident, I let myself linger in the limbo of wondering. In Egypt, after the blood rained down, then came the frogs, the lice, the locusts, and so on, until finally, in His final display of absolute power: the deaths of all the firstborn children. But really? In the front of my brain? I think Mrs. Daniel had a screen fall on her face that day, and yes, there was blood, but I doubt it was that bad. She had her life to live, a baby to take care of, and her life wasn't in the classroom with us—at least not all of it. Mrs. Daniels was a woman with a pixie cut who shopped in grocery stores and read books and—gasp—had sex with her husband (or with *someone* at any rate) and got herself in the family way. She's not mine to hold up in this moment of terror. I can let her go now.

I'm not convinced the human brain can be tidied like a purse, but I take comfort from the dumping, the categorizing, and the speaking of words that have gone unsaid. The brazen act of telling a story all the way through to the end.

NAKED UNDERNEATH OUR CLOTHES

A writing classroom is an intimate space, and so before I tell you about this night, years ago, when I was still what might classify as a young professor, a fresh transplant to Indiana soil from the wilds of the Pacific Northwest via the red clay of Alabama, and mother to a seven-month-old baby who took most of his nutrition from my body—before I bare all—I need to tell you something about what I was wearing. I'm sorry, but I do.

Between my voracious boy and the lack of maternity leave, I was shedding pounds like a calving glacier, dipping below my pre-pregnancy weight and still melting. Naturally, there was no time for clothes shopping, but this was a night class, three hours away from the baby, so I'd decided to dress up, albeit in ill-fitting clothes. I chose a substantial bra to harness breasts two letters further along in the alphabet song than they'd ever been before, a snuggish long-sleeved V-neck brown top, a blue and tan rayon skirt, sort of slippy, over caramel tights, and the pièce de résistance: super snazzy riding boots I'd ordered the previous year but hadn't been able to pull over my swollen calves. The boots were stepping out of the house for their very first time, and I may have been humming Nancy Sinatra to myself as I strode from the parking lot to my building, feeling like a real grown-up in actual clothes—and *boots*. To my knowledge, I didn't have a drop of spit-up or drool or pee on my person.

I wish I could tell you that what happened once I got to the classroom was one of those theatrical, innovative writing lessons wherein a well-prepared pedagogue stages a conflict in the classroom and afterward leads an illuminating discussion on eyewitness and memory. If I had any sense of propriety or self-protection, I would attempt now to recast the humiliating scene as such—but I would be lying. Despite my smart attire, I was insecure about everything and mad about most everything else.

For example, if I wasn't still fat, did I look saggy and soft? But if I was saggy and soft, was that anyone's goddamned business? Did I not have the right to be a mother in the academy? A postpartum, nursing mother in a real woman's body, pumping out milk and words and wisdom?

Was I smart enough? Did I belong here? Was I an impostor?

I had been doing a lot of thinking about breasts.

Also, I was tired.

Tonight was only our second meeting of the semester, and so my students and I were virtual strangers. Many months of limited social contact had diminished my confidence in having anything much to say beyond well-enunciated consonant sounds and color words, but I was, I told myself, a *professor*, and these boots were *made for walkin'*. So in I walked.

Introduction to Creative Nonfiction was held that semester on the ground level of the English department building, a brick monstrosity boasting a nearly windowless first floor that could serve as a tornado shelter. The effect was bunker-like. Strips of fluorescent lights glared down on the young, pink faces of the twenty or so would-be essayists who prior to our first class meeting had never heard the term "essay" without the descriptor "five-paragraph."

In the name of Socratic dialogue, I instructed the students to push their desks to the edges of the room, and after they compliantly screeched and clawed the little metal desk feet across the white tile (would it kill them to *pick up* the desks?), the fresh result was a horseshoe of smug or scared or bored faces all staring at me, waiting to see if I had anything to offer, anything at all, that might alleviate their self-consciousness, fear, and bottomless need.[1] And at the opening of the horseshoe, that empty space where all the luck can run out if you hang the shoe upside-down, was me, their rookie teacher—standing at the front of the hideous room, my own shining skin and brown top already smudged in chalk dust, with only a small table of carefully prepared notes and my black riding boots for protection. I remember thinking how *exposed* the notes looked spread across the laminate tabletop, how over-eager, how much *less smart* they appeared than when they'd been on the warm wood of our kitchen table, a sweet baby in my lap.

We were still working out together what the "creative" in "creative nonfiction" might mean if—as I was insisting—it *didn't* mean the author starts making stuff up when memory and research fail. Actually, the "nonfiction" part of our conversation hadn't gone particularly well either. Fallible, malleable memory. Levels of truth. True, truer, truest.

"How true is true enough? How do we ever know?" I challenged.

The students stared at me—as if they were *looking* at something. Despite my sturdy boots, I felt strangely unbalanced, but I pushed forward on a wave of good intentions and adrenaline.

"So," one young man in a baseball hat asked as we dutifully chalked lists of possibilities and considerations under the subheadings CREATIVE and NONFICTION, "I mean, how will *you* know whether what I write is true or not? How will you know the difference? I mean, basically, isn't nonfiction whatever I can trick you into believing?"

"Well," I said, taken aback. *Sources, sources.* "Yes. No. I mean *no.*" It occurs to me now that Baseball Cap and I were both trying desperately to "mean" something. I kept trying: "I mean, I want you to consider what Lee Gutkind, the godfather of creative nonfiction"—*Credibility, credibility*—"calls, umm, our contract with the reader. Our pledge to tell the truth to the best of our ability." *There.*

"So you *won't* know." Baseball Cap stretched his long legs out from beneath his tiny desk and leaned back in his chair, grinning as if he were the cat who swallowed the canary. No, as if he were the kid who'd left a mouse in my desk drawer and a glistening pile of fake vomit in my chair and I'd just discovered them both and screamed.

He was a smart kid. I'll give him that.

Essay. From the French, essai—*to try, to attempt, to take a stab,* I wrote on the chalkboard, tapping marks with my little wand, energetically pacing up at the front of the room, taking comfort in etymology and the smooth stick of chalk I gripped like a weapon.

The first essay up for discussion that night was "Out There" by Jo Ann Beard, about a solo, mid-divorce road trip up through Alabama during which Beard is pursued by a homicidal pervert from a backwoods gas station who tries to run her off the road, all the while making lewd gestures and screaming, "I'll *kill* you, I'll *kill* you" into the thick, hot Alabama air.

While I didn't share details of my own Deep South history with my students—my junior-faculty boundaries, despite my tell-all genre, were sharp—I had landed in Indiana after six years in central Alabama, where I'd been both an MFA student and an employee of the federal food stamps program, a job that involved driving on back roads so remote and chilling it seemed to me they were piping "Dueling Banjos" from the very trees. I had piloted my old gray Honda Accord to towns with names like Rainbow City, Opp, and Hueytown to visit gas stations, produce stands, and mom-and-pop grocers, where I'd pull out my clipboard, lanyard, and camera and get to work evaluating the store's eligibility to accept food stamps. My job was to count food items in each of the four food groups, taking photographs to confirm the existence of four dusty cans of Libby's fruit cocktail, two jars of Mott's apple-sauce, and three browning bananas, or a tilting box of Slim Jims and a short stack of potted meat food product.[2] The target was ten single-serving items per food group; after that, I could check the box, snap a photo, and stop counting. I wore khaki shorts, a polo shirt, and practical brown shoes.

Suffice to say, when Beard describes her "little convenience store, stuck out in the middle of nothing, a stain on the carpet," I *know* that store. I've fallen under the unbending gaze of the "various men, oldish and grungy" who stare at her "in a sullen way" while they chew. In fact, chances are excellent I've been in that very store checking off a wire rack of Lays chips for the Fruits & Vegetables column at the very counter where Beard stood to order that fateful cup of coffee on the day she was assaulted.

Beard was my sister. Beard could have been *me*. It's possible I shared air with the man in the lure-studded fishing hat who pursues Beard down the four-lane highway, screaming about what he wants to do to her through the hot air and the busted window. It's possible. Maybe on that day I just got lucky.[3]

Nearly a decade later, "Out There" is not the essay I'd have chosen for the second day of that intro class—both because of the violent subject matter and a fact I can see only in hindsight: reading this scene (basically the whole essay) still made me a little sick. I hadn't processed the vulnerability I'd felt each time I cut the engine in a parking lot, leaving what felt like the safety of my Honda to enter the buzzing, nearly deafening chorus of insects in the kudzu, listening as my own feet crunched the gravel, and then, with a deep, fortifying breath of chokingly hot air, pushing open the door of the next store on my list.[4] The smashing clang of the bell hanging from its shabby string was so *loud*—and then perfect silence as all the blue eyes, bluer than blue, swiveled in my direction, no sound at all until the whoosh of their collective held-in breath. *What the he-ell? Where did she come from?* And then the sound of my own voice speaking to whoever was behind the counter, in the position of authority we all grant to that rectangular strip in a place of retail, giving me away entirely: "Hi, I mean, he-eyy. My name is Jill Christman, and I'm working with the USDA food stamp program." Holding up my USDA ID in its plastic casing, couching everything I said in the positive. "I need to take a few pictures and make some notes. It'll just take me half an hour or so, and I'll try to stay out of the way . . ." *Damn Yankee.*

Christman. Christ, man. I had no business walking into those stores with my clipboard. I had no business leading a discussion on an essay with an intro class when I was still working through my own fear.

But I did—and there we are in a windowless classroom of the past, using up all the oxygen. Like Beard, "I feel sort of embarrassed for myself." We're out there, and this intense and dangerous tale is our first full essay up for discussion because my notes tell me I want to talk about Beard's artful use of present tense and how life—even at its most terrifying and hair-raising—doesn't come with plot. I ask them whether they're familiar with Freytag's Triangle—exposition, rising action, climax, and all the rest—and no one is, so I boot my way back to the chalkboard and draw it up there for them, dramatically, professorially, superimposing the familiar Cinderella story by way of illustration. This amuses and—I'm hoping—instructs them, although I'm somewhat disturbed by the fact that most of them are shouting out details that come from the Disney version with Lucifer the horrible cat creating obstacles and Cinderella's faithful mouse friends assisting in bringing about the happily-ever-after resolution. Never mind that. My neatly organized notes, fanned across the table, remind me that I want to look together at the way in which Beard orders information and uses foreshadowing to build tension. That's my goal. That's the subject on the table. Here is something we can learn, class.

I'm moving around a lot. I never sit down. I don't notice anything amiss, but I'm more in my mind than my body at this point. I wonder now, of course, if things were already beginning to slip.

Returning to the text, we read a bit from the moment Beard enters the gas station to buy some coffee. There is this sentence: "I swagger from the gas pump to the store, I don't even care if my boobs are roaming around inside my shirt, if my hair is a freaky snarl, if I look defiant and uppity."

Beard is not wearing a bra. I've never given this detail more than a passing thought, and even then, only to admire the way in which she gave agency and range to her *roaming* boobs. I entertain the vaguely inappropriate thought that my own boobs will be roaming nowhere soon, bound as they are by the industrial-strength nursing bra in such limited space. As soon as I turn my attention to my own breasts, they hear me. *Baby*, they whisper. *What about the baby? Do you think the baby might be getting hungry?* And then I feel an ache and a tingle. I feel them growing, straining the fabric of my brown V-neck top. *Not now*, I scold.

(Wait. Am I talking to my breasts in front of a class?)

The text. Stay with the text.

Earlier, Beard reports that she's going long-sleeved, naked underneath, instead of bikini top, because her "left arm is so brown it looks like a branch." This makes sense to me. I've been there. I've driven through Alabama in summer with only an open window and a spray bottle of water to serve as air conditioning. This strategy, born of desperation and busted A/C, is about as refreshing as putting your face at the end of the exhaust vent for your clothes dryer.

But on this night, my students are not thinking about the heat. They are thinking about Beard's braless breasts. They are thinking a *lot* about them.

To be fair, the student who will sprint past Baseball Cap and ascend to the role of antagonist in this story doesn't start it. A raven-haired, scornful girl who is sitting directly in my line of vision, at the top of the horseshoe, says she doesn't believe Beard was chased by this guy. "Seriously? Does stuff like that really happen?"

I tap on my open book with the flesh of my pointer finger and read aloud from the text: "He's telling me, amid the hot wind and poor Neil Young, what he wants to do to me. He wants to kill me. He's screaming and screaming, I can't look over. I stare straight ahead through the windshield, hands at ten and two."

And if it really did happen, Raven wants to know, can we *really* blame the husband at the end for not caring about Beard's story? "I mean, you know those girls who exaggerate everything? Make a big deal out of stuff just to get attention?" She sits back, point made, Baseball Cap–style, except she keeps her arms crossed tight against her chest, knees together.

The universe has tipped my horseshoe. The chalk cracks in my tightened fingers, and the floor shudders. My luck drains away. I can't remember what I say. Maybe nothing? Maybe I just point with my diminished chalk—palming the broken half—at the next raised hand, hoping I will be rescued by a kindred spirit, an astute close reader, or even just a veering distraction, a welcome change of lens.[5]

The hand I point to belongs to a young woman sitting about four feet to my left, quite close. In memory, I struggle to pull up the details of her personhood—curls, definitely curls, light-colored.[6] And I remember how earnest and serious she was, even before this night, following up after class with really specific questions about the syllabus and the days she already knew she'd be absent for a family trip to Florida that was planned *way* before she saw my absence policy. But mostly I remember how *close* she was to me physically. I take a few backward steps to increase the scope of the frame. What she does next does not help me to recover from Raven. Raven and Curls work together. A tag-team attack. All Baseball Cap has to do is sit back in his chair and enjoy the show.

Curls jumps into the ring: "Well. Okay. I mean, she wasn't wearing a bra, right? She *says* she wasn't wearing a bra. She went into that store without a bra on! She deserved it. Maybe if it did actually happen, she deserved it."

Now the room is honest-to-goodness whirling. My boots are no good to me in maintaining equilibrium. My response is immediate and uncomplicated.

I am livid. I feel my face get hot, and when my face gets hot, I get really, really red. I am a cherry lollipop on a boot stick. Okay, maybe my response *is* a little complicated. I am afraid to open my mouth. I am afraid of what might come out if I let my lips come apart and blow out warm air with words attached. I can see a script of possibilities ticker-taping across the dark screen of my inner forehead and none are appropriate. I see expletives. I see insults. There is name-calling. I see nothing I can actually say. I've had this job for about five minutes in the relative time of an academic career. I have *children* to support. Plus, we need to get through four essays tonight, and we're still on number one. It's a three-hour class, and I need to let them have a break. We all need a break. *Think think think. Breathe breathe breathe. Think-breathethinkbreathethink.* Maybe I don't need to let the full force of my women's-studies-self-defense-from-the-inside-out wrath loose on Curls, but neither can I let this kind of shit just hover in the blue air of *my* fucking classroom.

"Listen," I finally hear myself say in a shaking voice. "Listen. To. Me. This is not the point of today's discussion. But. Didn't I just say that our job in this class is not to critique the authors' lives? That we're thinking about the choices they make on the page, not the choices they make in their lives?"

The room is silent except for my breathing. I can feel my fury moving around inside my body like a physical presence, an undersized Tasmanian devil using my intestines as a hamster run.

Curls waits for me to finish.

"But," I continue, feeling as if I must, through sheer force of will alone, prevent my rage-filled body from spinning like a dervish, "let me say this before we continue our discussion: I should be able to walk down McKinley Avenue *naked*, completely naked, and be safe.[7] There is nothing I can do that makes me—or anybody, ever—*deserve* to be attacked. Nothing." And then, for good measure, I say again: "McKinley Avenue. Completely naked."

I'm looking hard at Curls, and she's looking right back, but the expression on her face is impossible to read. Why does she look so . . . self-satisfied?

I am so mad I want to cry.

Whatever transpires between my naked outburst and the break is lost to me. Certainly nothing good. My teaching notes tell me I emphasized *the breathless forward motion of the scene and the way in which, at the end, we come to understand what the story of being pursued on an Alabama highway is really all about and why the telling of that story is vital.* So maybe I said something like that before waving my hand and saying, "Go ahead. Ten minutes. Be back in ten. We have a lot to cover."

All the students leave the room—too quickly?—except for one. Curls. She approaches the table where I lean forward, fingertips tenting over my notes, trying to make some sense of what's left, how I'll get through it all, how I can recover what has already been lost.

"Professor Christman?"

It takes me a beat to recognize that this professor she is looking for is me. *Great,* I think. *Here we go.* I can still feel the current of anger flushing through my veins, but I am the teacher here. I am a grown-up. I have said what I needed to say, and now it is time to move on. I straighten and turn toward her.

Her eyes are on the floor, her expression enigmatic. She goes on: "I don't know how to tell you this . . ." Her voice fades.

"What?" I say, sharply, with an irritated flick of my hands I have been regretting for ten years. "What? What is it?" I am certain she has waited around to tell me something having to do with all those hussy women unlike her perfect self who just set themselves up, day after day, in their braless hussiness for sexual attack.

First, she points.

She points a steady finger at me, aiming just below my own most private of private parts, and then she turns her eyes up to meet mine, and she speaks: "Your skirt. Your skirt is falling off."

The moment freezes—my *what*? is *what*?—and then shifts into super slo-mo. Inside my mind I am screaming: *Noooooooooo . . .*

I break eye contact and look down. My God.

Oh. My. God.

The slippy skirt, so attractive in a professional way, so hip-skimming and floaty in a back-down-to-fighting-weight way when I was still safe at home or striding across the parking lot, has slipped. Not just a little. Too far. Much too far. There is a good eight-inch gap between the bottom hem of my top and the elastic waistband of my skirt, and in that eight-inch frame is my entire pelvis. There is a triangle of light flashing in the space formed by the bottom of my crotch, my honest-to-goodness vulva, and the waistband of my skirt. It's all there. All of it. Everything. Full-frontal, below-the-waist nudity—but for the caramel tights. So there's that. The tights both cursed—slippy on slippy? the reason I couldn't *feel* what was happening?—and blessed me. Some coverage. Something.

How long was it before I reached down with both hands and yanked my skirt up? Nano-seconds, right? It felt like forever. Eons of nakedness.

For the second time that night, I feel the heat in my face. The creep of blotchy red. "Thank you," is all I manage to say.

"You're welcome," she says, smiling. We are both embarrassed for me. I am that embarrassing. "I just thought you'd want to know." Her turn is a pivot, like the kind jazz dancers do, and her curls bounce behind her on the way out the door like Nellie Oleson's on *Little House* when she flounces back into her daddy's store for more candy, leaving a humiliated Laura on the street, dripping mud.[8]

I am Laura. If Laura were a skirtless hussy.

In the years that follow, when I tell the story of the night my skirt fell off during class, I make a joke of it: "What a missed opportunity! What a waste! When she said that—'Your skirt is falling off'—I should have just smiled like I'd planned it all along, like I was delighted she'd noticed, stepped out of what was hanging on of my skirt, whipped the slippy thing around my head like a lasso, and screamed, 'Damn straight! Take back the night, sister!'"

But I didn't. So I can't say that.

Here is the true ending.

When class resumed, the teacher made a request to all the assembled students: "Okay. So. In the future, should any piece of my clothing fall off during class, someone, anyone, should wave a hand in the air and alert me, okay?"

Afterward, the class continued through discussions of the three remaining essays and a first-memory exercise, all completely unmemorable, until finally, at 9:10 p.m., Completely Naked dismissed the class, packed up her notes and books, and walked back across the dark parking lot in her fancy boots, holding onto the waistband of her slippery skirt with one hand and her briefcase with the other, anxious to make it back home to her baby and take off her bra.

I thought that was the end of the story. But I was wrong.

Here is a question my students ask me again and again: "How long do you have to wait after something happens before you have the distance you need to write about it objectively?" The students who ask this question are almost always in pain. They're in the thick of a terrible betrayal or in the unflickering darkness of a depression, fumbling for the switch; they've too recently moved away from a house where there was alcoholism, abuse, neglect—or all three; someone they love, someone they *needed* to keep living, has just died; their bodies have been attacked (sometimes the assailant is themselves) or they're afraid if they swallow enough calories to sustain themselves no one will love them. In my twenty years of teaching, I have heard so many stories, and I hold onto these stories. I have come to understand that this is part of my job: to listen and receive the stories. So when my students ask, "How long do you have to wait?" I know, in part, they're asking for a number (two months, three years, four days), but I can't give them that. There's no way I could know.[9]

"It depends," I say. "Maybe you need to write about something five minutes after it happens, and that's going to capture details and nuance you won't be able to access two years later. But maybe you need those two years to figure out why something matters. So maybe you write something right away and then again two years later. Maybe what you write is two separate somethings because the consciousness you bring to bear on the events is everything—and those two years change your angle. Those two years change *you*. Or maybe you choose to fold over what you wrote on the day of the event with what you think two years later and it comes together to make one essay. It just depends. Of course, you can wait fifty years, and you'll never be 'objective.' The scope and distance of your subjectivity will change, but when we write essays, we are *always* subjective. That's the whole point." Here, I usually smile to make up for the fact that I'm not giving my students what they want to hear, the teachable key to unlocking the thing they need to say in a way that will take readers by the scruff of our necks and make us listen. We all want to be heard. And what they're really asking, usually, is: "Can I say this? I have a thing I really need to say. Can I say it?"

So sometimes I add this other true thing: "You are the only person on this planet who can tell your story. No one else can do it for you. So, if you don't do it, your story will never be told. If you have a story you need to tell, tell it. Write it down. You can always tell it again later if you want."

All the students with all their different faces and all their different hair and all their different names and all their different stories for the past ten years: "Can I say this?"

Me: "Yes."

The objectively disastrous skirt-falling-off Introduction to Creative Nonfiction class took place on a September evening nine years ago. That night, or the next day—very soon—I wrote down some of the details, recording mostly direct dialogue like, "I don't know how to tell you this." But then the file sat on my hard drive for years and years. Was that because I didn't have the "distance" to tell the story? Was I too embarrassed? Still angry? Conflicted? Or just otherwise occupied?

Now I wonder: How would I react today if the same scene played out in my classroom? I don't mean the skirt. I'd pull the skirt up, laugh, apologize, produce a safety pin from my purse, and deal with the situation. I'm a dance mom now, for heaven's sake. Wardrobe malfunctions fall into the category of fixable problems.

I'm talking about the bigger thing that happened that night. If a student tilted her hand and showed me her wounds. Think about it. What had already happened to Curls that compelled her to respond to Beard the way she did? What messages had she swallowed, digested, internalized? What does a young woman have to accept about *herself* in order to believe with such surety that the choice to not wear a bra because it's hot and uncomfortable could possibly equal a just punishment of rape or death?

I'm closer to getting it now. If this happened today, I don't think I would get angry. I definitely wouldn't feel compelled to stick to my lesson plan. I'd take the time to figure out what Curls was trying to tell me, tell all of us. Beard had opened up a portal for her, and when Curls tried to step through, I blocked the way. I missed my chance to help.[10]

I failed to understand that she was asking me a crucial question. I couldn't yet hear the question mark hiding at the end of her sentence. She was asking me something she needed to know, and I didn't answer. Nine years ago, while I stood in my boots at the front of that ugly classroom with my skirt slipping down my hips, Curls said, "Maybe if it did actually happen, she deserved it."

And I didn't realize she was asking for guidance. Instead, I heard only fighting words. I pushed back with everything in me that hadn't yet been healed from my own rape when I was a freshman, when I was the same age as Curls, when I wondered whether the invitation I'd accepted or the bikini I'd worn or the alcohol I'd swallowed that day had made the rape my fault, a secret I couldn't tell. I knew victim blaming when I heard it, and so, in a voice calibrated by rage, I had told Curls the truth: there is nothing any of us *does* to deserve sexual attack. But I couldn't hear the need below my students' judgment. I couldn't hear the buried fear Beard's essay evoked in me, carried up to Indiana from the steaming back roads of Alabama, the words of my own vulnerable self drowned out by the ringing of the cicadas. *It could have been me it could have been me it could have been me.*

If I could return to that room with those young writers, to that moment right after Curls said what she said—"Maybe if it did actually happen, she deserved it"—I would hear the question and I would hold her gaze. I would keep my face open to receive whatever else she needed to say, whatever else she needed to tell us all. I would move to pull up a desk to sit down—"Ooop! My skirt was falling down! Y'all should have said something!" Then I would laugh and adjust my clothing. The students would be relieved, and we'd screech the little desk feet across the floor to tighten our horseshoe into a circle. "Okay," I would say—without edge, without anger, leaving my lesson plan behind. "Why? Let's talk about what's here that makes us want to distrust and cast judgment on Beard."

And then I would listen.

Notes

1. Really, isn't this what we all want from our English classes when we're eighteen? Someone to actually see us and say: "I hear you. You're smart. You matter. *You're okay.* It's all going to be okay."
2. It is a seldom-observed fact that the first ingredient in the majority of your potted meats is "mechanically separated chicken," and I cannot

tell you how many hot road hours I spent pondering the specifics of how those poor chickens died. I mean, it's one thing to be separated by hand—I guess—but to be *mechanically* separated? What would that entail? Something like a blender? Robotic gloves? What the hell?

3. Pedagogical Rule: Don't teach literature you love with the goal of having your students join you in your passion. This way lurks disappointment and resentment. A notable exception to this rule, somewhat ironically, is Beard's own "The Fourth State of Matter," from the same collection. I love it. My students love it. I can't stop reading and teaching that mind-blowingly necessary essay. If you've never read it (and if you're the kind of person who would be reading *this* essay, that strikes me as damn unlikely), finish this one and then make haste to *The Boys of My Youth* by Jo Ann Beard.

4. Amplified, cinematic gravel-crunching, like the sound you hear in the theater over the gustatory mawing of popcorn and tearing of Twizzlers wrappers when the stupid college student from Oregon is walking into the convenience store in the middle of nowhere alone and you're thinking: *Do not go in there.*

5. Pedagogical Rule: Never let them see your fear.

6. Random fact: Teachers require different hair colors, cuts, and styles to distinguish students from one another, especially early on. We're like prosopagnosiacs that way. A student—who herself cannot remember faces—taught me this.

7. McKinley Avenue is the main artery on Ball State University's campus, the crowning feature of which is a bell tower rising 150 erect feet and featuring forty-eight bells chiming out the Westminster Quarters. If you want to see or be seen on our campus, this is the road you choose.

8. Years after *Little House on the Prairie* went off the air, the actress who played Nellie, Alison Arngrim, resurrected her career with the deliciously titled one-woman show and best-selling book *Confessions of a Prairie Bitch: How I Survived Nellie Oleson and Learned to Love Being Hated.* Arngrim refused to be shamed.

9. I say "maybe" a lot when I'm teaching. The longer I'm in the classroom, the less sure I am of anything, and the more willing I am to travel into uncertainties. This is not a bad thing.

10. Teaching is hard in many of the same ways writing is hard: you have to be prepared, and you have to be willing to let go of your plan and follow the surprises; you have to be brave; you have to know the rules—and when to break them. Some days, teaching is like a dance, and others can feel more like a wrestling match. Either way, you might come out sweating.

SPINNING

Spinning. I am spinning. Not like my six-year-old son whirling, spinning for that moment when equilibrium flies away like fluff from a dandelion and he lurches sideways, goes down grinning. Not like a field full of tripping Dead fans, flailing and twirling, open palms to the sky, ready to receive anything. Not even like my own 4 a.m. mind, turning over worries as wide-ranging as the lack of storage in the kids' room to the essay in need of a better ending.

No. This is an exercise class where we churn the pedals as hard as we can and still go nowhere. The shining flywheels on our stationary bikes are the only things *actually* spinning. Also, at the YMCA in Muncie, Indiana, where I spin at 8 a.m. on Mondays, Wednesdays, and Fridays, it's officially called "Y-cycling" because that other name is registered to the folks who make a particular brand of bike—too bad—and our bikes are Keiser, which I think about more often than I should because it's stamped in red on the back of each black vinyl seat, so when I'm looking at someone's Lycra-clad keister, wiggling in an exercising sort of way above the seat, pumping out "Jumpin' Jack Flash" or taking names on the fast flats during "Friday I'm in Love," my comrade's fanny is actually labeled "Keiser," which is the sort of thing that makes me smile at 8 a.m. when I've had just the one cup of coffee and I'm starting to sweat out even that.

The room where we ride could not be more ugly. It's on the top level of the Y and has a windowless, low-hanging drop ceiling made up of particle-board panels that look as if they were pressed in the heyday of asbestos. Because the evening instructor likes to conduct her class in semi-darkness with no overhead lights, she had the ceiling painted black and the rear wall a deep-bruise purple. I'm pretty sure this is what interior decorators would recommend if you were going for a kind of apocalyptic ambiance—foreshortened sky, the world pressing down on you—but I've heard the evening instructor say she just doesn't like to ride with the lights on. She doesn't like the way her skin looks, sweating, under the fluorescents. The remaining three walls are a dull nicotine yellow. Thirty bikes all face the small platform with the instructor's bike and the red kick bag that serves as a side table for her iPod. At 8 a.m., we ride under the humming ultraviolet rectangles cut into the low ceiling—our false sun. Two giant mirrors at the front of the room create the illusion that we are riding toward ourselves.

What if we could do that? I wonder some mornings. *Pedal hard and arrive at ourselves? What would we do? What would we say?*

I can imagine prettier places to ride, but I cannot imagine a nicer group of people. I'd say we're an even mix of retired folks, stay-at-home moms, and professionals with weird schedules (professors, like me, and a few doctors and nurses); the morning class doesn't attract college students. It's too early, for one thing. We exchange pleasantries about the early hour and the weather as we prepare ourselves and our bikes for the ride.

"Cold enough for you this morning?"

"Get the kids to school on time?"

"Hey, are those new glasses, Jill?"

Sometimes, when the friendly greetings kick in, I hear the *Cheers* song jingling in my head as I drape my rough Y-issued towel over the smooth black handles of the bike, twist the thick knobs and adjust the seat bar, trade out clogs for Velcroed cycling shoes, swing my leg over—always from the left, as if I'm still back in the West, mounting a horse—and clip into the pedals.

This is nice, I always think. I am grateful for this ugly room and its beautiful people. And if it weren't for what happens when human beings strip off their outer layers, raise their butts in the air, and ride hard until their thighs burn and their brains warm and open to a place where the right song has the power to open a portal to another time, this might just be a sweet story about unexpected community in a small midwestern city.

Our instructor is beautiful—sleek like a racehorse, blond and manicured but still natural in a Christie Brinkley CoverGirl-clean kind of a way. Speaking of which, she has a soft spot for Billy Joel, too, but then, there's no way to pin down Celeste's eclectic musical tastes, which range from new country to hair band, Motown to speed metal, nineties grunge to contemporary Christian. One moment, we'll be sprinting to the hip, urgent strains of a floppy-haired alternative dude, and the next, rolling upward in a slow climb, tension cranked up to eighteen or nineteen, pulled up by the dulcet crooning of a coffeehouse songstress, and then, I don't know, John Denver or the Georgia Satellites, for heaven's sake, will burst from the speakers, and we'll go either *Rocky Mountain high-iiigh* or slap down sexual advances from another time and place, the retired teachers chiming in with grins and shouts—"Don't hand me no lines and keep your hands to yourself!"

Whether Celeste engages this range because her tastes are really that wide or because she wants to make everyone happy—if only for a moment—I'm not sure, but I can attest that it's always interesting in a mind-travel kind of way. My mother listened to John Denver when she layered sauce and lasagna noodles in the kitchen. My high school boyfriend sang along to the Satellites when he picked me up from school on Friday afternoons in his Jeep, spinning gravel through his tires as he sped out of the back lot, a beer already sweating in its aluminum between his thighs.

Sometimes, when I spin, I need to shake off the images that rise up with the change of song—remember what year it is, where I am, who loves me. I concentrate on tightening the muscles in my core, holding my back straight, keeping a slight bend in my elbows, wiping a drip of sweat from my blurring eye.

I want to give you this background, make sure you are clear on the setting, before I get to the part that's harder to hear, almost impossible to believe—except I do believe it. There was a time when I wouldn't have believed. There was a time when I would have said there are things that happen and things that don't, and we know the difference. People die and go away, for example. People die and are gone.

I'm forty-four now, double fours, and I am telling you what I *do* know so that, together, we might push our fingers into the unknowable, dig about for the juiciest plum.

The plumbing of mysteries requires absolute clarity and utter chaos.

When I was nineteen years old, I went home with my best college friend, Diane, a friend who is *still* my best friend, for Thanksgiving. We got there late at night, driving down from Oregon to California with her two little girls sleeping in the back, and everyone was in bed when we arrived. So it wasn't until Thanksgiving morning that I first saw her brother, Colin—whom I'd heard about but not considered, not really, as I'd never really considered death or dying or the hereafter. Wearing cut-off jeans and a t-shirt, my bed-messed hair skewered in place with a pencil, I was ascending the spiral staircase, following the sound of voices and the smell of coffee. It doesn't seem possible that I truly remember the quality of light in this first picture of Colin, but I feel as if I do. Thanksgiving morning, late November, but it was northern California, San Rafael, and later in the day we would take a hike with the dog across a sunny mountaintop, so maybe I'm not too far off when I tell you the light was golden, when I tell you that in my first vision of Colin he was gleaming, godlike. Too beautiful to be real. I remember what he was wearing, too: faded Levi's. Nothing else. *My God.*

One bronzed arm arced across the squirming body of his four-year-old niece, Haley, who was all baby-powder smell in soft pajamas, his lean muscles flexing and holding her up. The fingers of his other hand—long, guitar-playing fingers—curled around a coffee mug. Here was everything I wanted from a morning, posed at the top of the stairs.

I can't speak to the love—like the golden light, that seems unfair to claim outright (although I'd like to do that and have it be true)—but the lust was immediate. Later, Colin and I would discuss how the attraction between us actually buzzed. Our lust made a *sound*. Maybe it was the element of surprise. Maybe it was two spinning spheres coming close enough to touch, locking in—a kind of Venn diagram of desire, with me and Colin at the intersection, drooling.

"Hi," I said, loading the word with more sex than I intended.

"Hi," he answered, bending his knees and lowering Haley's feet toward the solid ground without unlocking the grip of his eyes from mine. His eyelashes were long, like a girl's, his hair so dark it was almost black, everything about him disheveled. Everything about him asking to be taken back to bed.

I swallowed and licked my lips. "I'm Jill," I said. Haley's swinging feet gained purchase, and she trotted down the hall, toward kitchen noises. We were alone at the top of the stairs.

"I figured. I'm Colin."

"Yeah. I figured. Diane told me about you. Sort of."

"Yeah. Me too. I mean, she did too. Told me about you." He paused. "Sort of. Umm. Coffee?"

"That'd be great."

It was Thanksgiving Day 1988, only 8:30 a.m., and Colin and I were already feeling grateful. By midnight, Diane would hear a ruckus and think that somebody was spinning an unbalanced load in the washer. This wasn't like me, and it wasn't like Colin, either, this shameless leap into the sheets, his bed made up on the floor of his mother's office and me in it, but we both seemed to know our time was set to expire, the sand in our hourglass was running.

Before the next Thanksgiving, Colin would be dead—killed at an intersection in Tillamook, Oregon, burned to dust and then taken home, scattered in the California hills where he'd raced with his dogs and learned to rope calves. Before I turned twenty-one, I would be a kind of widow, spinning.

I would need a thousand pages to clearly explain all that has gone down in the world's spinning from the night Colin stepped off this earth and into the never-never and I stayed behind to build a life worthy of the way he had loved me. Before Colin, I'd been a girl on the edge of survival: smart but broken, ambitious but wounded, dancing along the dark edge of despair, hoping someone would notice—and then, like a miracle, someone did. I was only nineteen when we met, and Colin was just two years older. He loved me as no one before him ever had, with the kind of love that made me love myself.

By the time we locked eyes at the top of that spiral staircase, I'd been suffering from bulimia for seven years. Colin loved me into stopping—it seems impossible, but it's true—and when he died, I thought, *Why not go back? Slip off the wagon. What difference does it make now?* But I heard Colin's voice in my head—speaking sharply, for an angel, but also sadly, sensibly. He said, *I don't even have a body anymore, Jill.* I was in the bathtub, watching my hands float like sea creatures in the water, wholly separate. I heard every word clearly, and I knew what he meant. I knew I had to take care of my body. He couldn't do it, so I would.

"Take off two," Celeste instructs. "Take a breather," she says. "Get some water."

We do. We drink, we wipe sweat off our faces, and for the millionth time I wish I were the kind of person who brought her own fluffy towel from home and didn't scratch at my forehead with the over-bleached and still dingy towels that have wiped the faces (and God knows what else) of so many other human bodies. For about five seconds, we listen to the sound of our collective breathing, the gulping of water, our stainless-steel bottles clanging back into the curves molded for them on the handlebar posts. Tom Petty starts crooning. *She's a goooood girl, loves her mama . . .*

"Okay. Breather over," Celeste says through her headset. "Add three. We're going up a big hill."

I stand up in my pedals and put my weight into my legs, wiggle my toes to make sure they're not curling, flatten my feet. Proper alignment.

"Free Fallin'" came out in 1989, the summer before Colin died, the summer Colin took care of me. I wouldn't have been able to imagine a world without him, but then, it never occurred to me to try. Why would I? I knew he would always be there.

We lived in Washington State, in a generic apartment complex close to Sea-Tac so that Colin could easily get to his nightly job, babysitting British advertising blimps parked on the airfield. Every hour, he checked the pressure and moved a lever up or down, and in between, he sat in a trailer in the diffused light of the giant, needy glowworms and played his guitar. Joe Satriani. Eric Clapton. Jimi Hendrix. And, that summer, Tom Petty. *Loves Jeee-sus and America, too.*

I've seen pictures of Colin on the airfield, gripping a long rope draped around his waist, the floating blimp as placid as a grazing manatee bobbing in the weeds, but I never visited him with his tethered charges, because I didn't have airport clearance. Something about the fact that he was alone on the night shift, coupled with the weirdness of light-up marketing airships with their fluctuating gasses and temperaments, and, of course, the image of Colin out there with his guitar, sending his song out into all that silent midnight air, seemed so *romantic.*

Colin preferred to call the blimps *dirigibles.* Dirigible. Such a good word.

After Colin was gone, I was traveling through Central America, grieving hard, and I met this man, a merchant marine, much older—who knew? who cared? maybe thirty-five to my twenty—and the way he seduced me, if you could call it that, if there's seduction involved in offering the ruined girl I was one night to pretend she wasn't alone, was the image he spun for me of himself on deck at night, far out at sea, alone with all that shimmering blackness, playing his harmonica for the stars and the fishes. That was the picture I held in my mind when he took me back to his tiny room in the pension, a room just big enough for the bed, and tried to do what I couldn't, in the end, let him finish. It was too sad. Too wrong. *Free fallin'.* The merchant marine and his harmonica couldn't fix what was broken in me, and so we went to a bar to drink tequila. I tapped my glass on the bar with too much force, taking a chunk out of the lip, but I was too far gone to notice, and before my sailor friend could reach out his hand to stop me, I tilted the burning amber down my throat, glass shards and all.

In the early months after Colin died, I made a study of dreaming. I read books about lucid dreaming; set my alarm for odd hours, hoping to catch us together; counted the fingers on my hands in waking and dreaming, with an eye peeled for that extra digit or six; lulled myself to sleep muttering, "I will know I'm dreaming, I will know I'm dreaming . . ." It's hard to explain how logical this was to me. If I could not be with Colin here in this earthly realm—this was the language I'd adopted—well, then, I would go to where he was.

I would find him.

I wouldn't believe this if it hadn't happened to me. I was half mad—or more—from grief. I could barely get up in the morning after remembering: *Colin's dead.* I didn't want to live in this world without him. I believed what I needed to believe, saw what I needed to see, in order to survive, but weird shit happened. For example, it became normal for Colin to inhabit electrical devices.

Spinning

For a few months, it felt as if the world had been rewired just for me. As I walked by streetlights, they would blink on and off. When I entered my house, the lamp in the living room would turn on by itself. *Hello, sweetheart.* Or there was the night I was awoken from sleep by a cat jumping onto my legs and exerting a warm and gentle pressure—*I love you*, the pressure said. *I'm okay.* There was no cat.

And yet, as the months wore on, despite the hours I spent on the floor with my back leaning against the cases in the New Age bookstore, reading about lucid dreaming, breathing in sandalwood, and watching the crystals flash and dance on the rug, I never quite got there. I never reunited with Colin in my dreams.

Well, that's not exactly true. I developed to a point where I knew I was dreaming when I was dreaming, but Colin was never ready to cooperate; it seemed that he was *not* dreaming. (Approaching all this from the spiritual perspective, would everything be backward? Did Colin need a different handbook?) He would appear in my dreams, but even there, in what was supposed to be the deepest place of my imagination, a borderless land of possibility, he was always dead. Unreachable.

Hold me, I would beg, showing him my hands, weeping, entreating him to see how I was broken and alone in a way that required his intervention, even if it was against the rules of the angels. *I'm sorry*, he'd say, looking sorry. Then, more brightly, *You're going to be okay. I'm okay. I can't touch you. I don't have a body.*

But this is a dream, I'd protest. Wasn't anything possible in a dream? Couldn't two people separated by death come together in a dream?

Apparently not. Apparently, it was against the new rules. This alternately broke my heart and pissed me off. *Please!* I'd beg. *I'm dreaming. Do you have to be dead everywhere?*

Colin has been gone for twenty-four years now. I'm not a young woman anymore. I wouldn't be caught dead—what a phrase, as

191

if you can surprise these people—in cut-off jeans like the ones I was wearing on the morning we met, but I do still sometimes bind my long hair with a pencil, in a pinch. Also, and significantly, I've been married for eleven years to another love of my life—proving we're not all limited to just one—and my husband, Mark, and I have our spinning six-year-old, Henry, and his ten-year-old sister, Ella. I am wildly in love with these people I get to live with, and I am so grateful—but I worry. Not *but*. And. *And* I worry. Having known how someone we love can be there and then not be there—crash, poof, gone—I watch my beloveds carefully, even as I try not to make them afraid.

If Colin and I had married and started a family, as we planned, our oldest child would be twenty-two or twenty-three—which is to say, our oldest kid would be older than Colin was when he died. Which is to say, I am old enough to be *mother* to the young man Colin was when he died.

So, that's who I was last week when Colin—finally!—stepped down from wherever he has been, fully fleshed and pedal-stopping handsome, and paid me a visit.

If I'd known Colin was going to show up, I would have made a mental note of what was playing when he walked in. If I could remember the portal, would I be able to find it again? More to the point, perhaps: would I want to? Let's say it was Meatloaf's "Paradise by the Dashboard Lights." He loved that song. We used to sing it in two parts. No. If Meatloaf had been playing when Colin strolled into my spinning class, I would have fallen off my stationary bicycle. Plus, I don't think I've ever heard Celeste play Meatloaf.

No. I think it was "Come Sail Away," that ubiquitous Styx song on every cycling instructor's spin list. Yes. That was the song.

On the day Colin came to see me—walked in, on *legs*—my cycling buddies and I were riding nowhere up near the rooftop of the YMCA while an early March snowstorm blew outside, snowflakes spinning in unlovely whorls in the air above the frigid parking lot. It was the first day of spring break, and Mark and I were planning to drive south with the kids to spend a couple of nights in a Brown County cabin. I was worrying about the weather and the roads. Despite the storm outside, our purple room under the warehouse eaves was hot, hot, hot. The roaring swamp fans were blowing, and I was a sweating, shining writing professor in her midforties wearing a spiffy black yoga top and stretchy pants, trying to fend off gravity's pull for a few more years. Styx was just about to take us from crooning ballad to driving guitars, and I was settling into my legs to get ready for the surge.

Because I am in the front row, riding straight into my own reflection, I see the guy in the mirror only. I see him stride in with long steps, long after class has started, and choose a bike two rows back, over my right shoulder. Watching the curve of his back as he bends over to adjust his bike, I feel a strange jolt of recognition. I try to concentrate on Celeste: "Give me two more, two more numbers." I move the lever forward with my thumb and rise up, pushing my weight and my power into my legs. The next time I look up, the stranger is on the bike, and I can see his face—and his face is Colin's face.

The stranger is not a stranger. He is Colin, and he is fewer than eight feet behind me, standing in his pedals. All the parts—olive skin, Roman nose, long dark lashes, deep-brown eyes, thick brows, disheveled hair—but also: Colinness. Playful. Kind. A little cocky.

I gasp. Audibly. Right into the silence at the end of the song. Right into the next moment when I could not, do not, look away. I try to look away because even in my shock I know it is too weird. What would it appear I was doing? Ogling this hot guy young enough to be my son? How would I explain my dropped jaw and greedy eyes? And to whom?

But then the doppelgänger is pulling off his sweatshirt, and when he does, his t-shirt pulls up, too, and his torso is Colin's, his chest is Colin's, the long line between the deltoid and the triceps, curving around, a shadow, into the bulge of the bicep, is Colin's. As a forty-four-year-old woman gawking at the body of my twenty-two-year-old lover, I am grateful for the trick of the mirror, the way in which the line of my sight would be obscured, because what I am doing is unseemly. What I am doing isn't right, but I can't help myself. I can't look away. I can't tell you whether I felt older than I ever have, or younger. What would I have done if this had happened twenty-four years ago, in the months of spinning grief after the accident? I don't even have to ask that question. I would have leapt off my bike. Right then and there. I would have looked him in the eyes, no mirror in between, and said: "You're back. You came back. Thank God. I knew you wouldn't leave me."

Now, it is too late for that. The Counting Crows kick in. "Rain King." Heaven and a black-winged bird.

Two weeks after Colin died, I felt the cat who wasn't there leap onto my legs and tell me in Colin's voice—which wasn't spoken but was clear and strong in my head—that I was loved. He was okay and I would be okay, Colin told me. I was wide awake and sitting up in bed and this is what I heard. Logically, of course, visits from angels make no earthly sense, but these moments are the closest I've come to knowing for sure that there's more to this life than logic.

There's love, for one thing. Does love make any sense?

Colin knew he was going to die. He didn't tell me, but he told my mother in the month before the accident. I must have been off at class, and Colin was helping her split and stack the wood from a fallen tree in her backyard. After the accident, my mother told me about their conversation, how each time they'd passed each other with their arms loaded, he'd offered advice on how to take care of me. I was fragile then, and he wanted to make sure my mother knew how to handle the bulimia. He told her, "You'll have to be the one to help her when I'm gone." My mother was confused—where was he going?—but after Colin was killed, she told me she realized he was trying to tell her he wouldn't be around much longer. Time was almost up.

Afterward, hearing my mother's story, I was mad. Wouldn't this have been good information for me to have as well? If he'd told me, couldn't we have worked together to change the course of the future? How hard would it have been for him not to get in the van that night to run for pizza? Or just to have paused to tie his shoe before he climbed into the back? That's all it would have taken. Twenty seconds, and this would be a different story. Twenty seconds this way or that, and I would not be riding a stationary bicycle in a stifling room in a city they call Middletown, USA. I would not be worrying about the snow on the highway— or my children.

I can't remember where we got the lucky rock or how this smooth chunk of hematite, surprisingly heavy, became part of Colin's daily uniform, but I know it happened before the end of our first and last summer together because I remember him kissing me good-bye, extracting my promise that I'd be good to myself, and then patting his front right pocket to make sure his lucky rock was there before he got into the car and drove to the airfield. When he was home, Colin kept the shining, silver rock on the bureau next to his wallet, keys, and watch. After he fastened his belt, I'd often see him weigh the heft of the stone in his palm, stroke the curve of the rock's underbelly, and then slip it in his pocket. Colin liked to have something to touch.

I had a matching lucky rock, but I didn't carry mine. Now the stones are together in the closet in a box marked "Colin" with a Sharpie. I sometimes wonder why Colin thought he needed extra luck. Maybe his death wasn't the final stroke of bad luck. Maybe there are worse things than death.

"Push into those legs," Celeste commands, scanning the room. Then her eyes land on mine. "Push. Make those legs work. This should leave a mark."

When my daughter, Ella, was a toddler, she used to say, "Hold me!" The pitch of her plea, and the way in which she rounded and pulled that first word, sliding down it to land on the "me," was more Baptist preacher than two-year-old. She said it a lot. When I was leaving her somewhere, or picking her up from a place I'd left her. When she was scared by a bigger-than-usual dog or overwhelmed by a large crowd of people. When we stepped onto an elevator and the doors slid shut like a hungry maw. When she was nervous or angry or tired or lonely. "Hold me, Mama! Hold me." And because we were both here on this earth, flesh-bound and hearts beating, I always did. I always did.

I got Colin's hematite back from the man at the funeral home, a plastic man in a plastic suit, with motionless hair like the kind my kids snap off and on their LEGO minifigures. The white paper bag he put into my hands was flimsy, take-out-order cheap, and I remember its contents—*his personal effects*—more by touch than by sight, as if I'd gone blind. My shaking fingers fumbled around in the debris, dirt, and rough rocks and found the hematite, smooth and warm. I pulled the stone from the bag and stared at it in my hand, my own sad face—whose face?—reflected back in the polished surface. A mirror of a rock.

In the fold of his wallet, the leather worn into a smooth shell by the tides of his body, there was a wad of cash, probably his per diem for the week, probably the stash he would have dug into that night if he and his workmates had made it to the pizza place for a late dinner. The money was still wet. Blood had soaked through the bend in the wallet, the crack, and drenched the money. I got some on my fingers and heard someone screaming.

I did not recognize the shrieks as my own.

In time, the blood dried, turning darker red, and eventually a kind of dirty black, and finally Colin's money withered into something I could spend without the cashier thinking: *Here is the blood-soaked money of a man far too young who died in a fiery crash.* Diane and I took the wad in an envelope and bought lunch at Colin's favorite restaurant, a place where he liked the soup and the fancy black-bottom pie. We meant it as a gesture of celebration, healthy grieving, but the toasted baguette stuck in my throat; the pie's cream was too thick for swallowing.

In the bag, I also found the ring I'd given to him, silver, adorned with tiny bumps around the outside, too big for me to wear, so I slipped it onto my watchband. It wore divots into my wrist that I rubbed with my finger, a kind of Braille to read who we were before the accident, before all I had left to hold was a ring, a rock, and a bloody wallet.

When will I stop? It's been twenty-four years. I am in what I'm hoping is the dead middle of an extraordinary and lucky life. I have written and written and written the story of our love, the sad tale of our loss. Enough is enough. What more is there to say? And then Colin steps out of the blowing spring snow and shows up in my spinning class. What is he doing here? Has he come to warn me? Am I supposed to warn *him*? And, if so, of what? Why now?

Don't look, Jill, I command myself. *Don't look*. But seriously: What am I supposed to do? What would *you* do if your long-dead lover showed up in your cycling class? I look.

And then things get silly. My spinning friends start singing along with Hall & Oates; particularly boisterous is the woman who brought us all tambourines to shake as we pedaled at Christmastime, hanging a chiming wooden ring on each bike like a gift. *She's a maaaaa-aneater!* And her buddy, a woman who wears *two* terry cloth headbands, one around her forehead, *Flashdance*-style, and another one around her neck—a style all her own—joins in: *Whoa-oh here she comes, watch out, boy, she'll chew you up!*

A retired biology teacher a couple bikes down gets caught up in the fun. He belts out the chorus—"She's an anteater!"—with all he has, apparently not thinking his misheard lyrics at all odd, that our boy should watch out for the approaching long-snouted anteater. It's all so weird.

I look at Colin in the mirror, and there he is, pedaling away. He's wearing a red New York Fitness shirt with the sleeves cut off at the top of the shoulders, just like the real Colin, my Colin, used to do to his workout shirts, and when he starts to sweat, riding hard behind me as if he can catch up, he grabs the front of his shirt and pulls it up to mop his face. Another gesture of Colin's. A glimpse of flat stomach, hairless, a trickle of sweat.

What is Colin doing here? What has he come to tell me?

Because I'm seeing all of this in the mirror, everything behind me, and also because I'm feeling woozy from exertion, this new reality is wavering, undulating. I feel as if I'm looking back in time, back through memory to a place where Colin is alive and biking, alive and sweating. Like we've come here this morning to ride together. Like this is just a normal thing we do.

What is this feeling? Elation? Terror? Finally, after twenty-four years, Colin has defied the rules of angels, he's come *back*, and I don't know what to do.

Again, Celeste looks right at me. Has she noticed something wrong? "Don't slow it down," she challenges. For all I know, I've stopped pedaling altogether and I deserve a chastising from the teacher. "Bring it up two more." And we all reach down and push the black levers forward with our palms. "Strong legs, strong heart!" My own heart feels weak, sick, and I would stop, but if I did, I would have to walk right past Colin's doppelgänger to get out of the room, and if I did that, what would my face reveal?

Surely this is just a kid who came to the Y to get some exercise before class. I have never seen him here before, and although I don't know it now, I will never see him again. He has come to the Y this one morning out of hundreds of mornings, and he will never come back. Never. That's not the way real, living people with YMCA memberships use the Y. Real, living people with Y memberships come *back* to the Y, morning after morning, week after week.

But not Colin. He has come to ride with me just this single snowy day.

Between songs, I take a deep drink from my water bottle, letting the cool steel of the lip ground me to this earth.

What is he doing here? Ridiculously, I feel as if this is something I *could* figure out. What's the appropriate response for me here? Am I supposed to believe? Not believe? Am I supposed to study him, smile at him, *talk* to him—or duck my head and sneak out? Sexual attraction is not the right word for what I feel. No. What I am talking about is the complete obliteration of time.

This is not a Colin who's been computer enhanced to age from the moment before impact in 1989 to 2014. This is Colin *then*, and if this is true and possible, as my every sense seems to be telling me it is, then who am I, and how old? My feelings for the man I'd loved in the restless, complete way of twenty-year-olds, and lost with the same intensity, were dug up and cracked open by Colin's reappearance, a flung-open time capsule of impossibility spilling onto a midwestern landscape that had felt solid—until this morning.

I check the mirror again, fully expecting to see the girl I once was. If I squint my eyes until the stars come, I can see her there, and then I feel another flash of fear. If Colin has come back to warn me, does that mean my babies are in danger?

Maybe we shouldn't make the drive to Brown County—in the snow, with the kids. Mark and I were worried that the roads might be too bad to make the trip. Maybe Colin has come to tell me not to go, to warn me it's not safe. The kids. Maybe all these years he's been keeping his distance—he's dead, after all—but also keeping watch. Just in case. Maybe today required intervention, and Colin decided to break the rules of angels.

We're doing jumps. Up for eight, down for eight. My heart is racing and I feel hot. Too hot. *I should stop*, I think. I'm going to pass out. But that would give me away, so I don't. I keep going.

Celeste pumps her thumb twice toward the ceiling. "Add two more if you can. This is how you make change in your body. This shouldn't be comfortable."

It isn't. Not remotely. I add two.

I look up into the mirror and Colin is still there, pedaling hard, standing taller in the stirrups than anyone else in the class. I could swear that boy has a halo, a light on his head. What am I going to say to him? Maybe nothing. Probably nothing.

"Don't fight it," Celeste says. "Ride it."

The last song is "Everybody Have Fun Tonight" or "Ticket to Ride" or "Blinded by the Light." I can't remember exactly, maybe because I can't really hear. There's a roar in my ears. I can hear my own blood pumping, spinning through my circulatory system, and it's so loud, as if I've covered both ears with conch shells. I am deafened by the sonic ocean of my own wet body.

I know I have about three more minutes to look at him and decide what to do. How can he look so much like Colin and not *be* Colin? In German, *doppelgänger* means "double walker" or "double goer," and this shadow self can be a harbinger of mortal danger—but Colin is already dead. It's too late for all that now. I steal a look in the mirror. I want to catch his eye without looking like I'm trying to catch his eye. My heart burns with effort and a fresh stab of loss. *Oh, Colin*, I think. *I love you. I'm sorry.* But even as I feel sorry with all of my body, worked past the point of exhaustion, I don't know *why* I'm sorry. I don't know what I'm sorry *for*.

Because I got to live a full life and he didn't? Am I sorry because he saved me and I could not, did not, save *him*? Maybe I am sorry because if he *has* come back, if this *is* Colin, flesh and blood, come back to find me in Muncie, Indiana, I will not be able to love him like I did. Not in the same way.

With a jolt, I realize I have broken my promise. I am *not* waiting for Colin, as I always said I would be, no matter what. I have Mark and the kids.

Am I sorry because I don't know what I would be to him if he did come back? Would I make him up a room on the second floor with Henry and Ella? Make sure he finished his college degree? Would I be his *mother*? But Colin already has a mother who has been missing him just the way he is. She would take him back, and I . . . I don't know.

I'm sorry, Colin.

I love to set a quarter spinning on a smooth table. The quarter is only a coin, twenty-five cents, something I could spend on twelve minutes of parking or a gumball, but when I balance it vertically with one finger and flick it hard on its edge with another, the quarter dervishes into a cyclonic blur, skidding across the table. Why is it so satisfying to watch this silver spinning? The quarter changes. While it spins, the quarter is not a quarter. Its borders disappear—but you can't touch it. You want to. You want to touch it, to feel with your finger what it is to spin your way to transformation, but if you do, the quarter drops to the table, regains its ridged edges. Done. The quarter is once again a quarter.

And then there are the Sufis, whirling themselves to another spiritual plane altogether. I have seen these dervishes in videos, right palm up toward God, left palm down, grounding them to the earth, one leg—always the left—the stable pole of their whirling, centered like a ballerina's in a jewelry box when the lid tips back, while the other scooter-kicks in a fast circle, around and around, the Sufi's head canted toward his shoulder in ecstasy.

No. Too many distracting images—the jewelry box, the scooter. As usual, I am missing the point. Around and around and around go the Sufi dervishes, around and around, until their gowns fill with air and fly up in perfect circles, spinning away ego and desire, spinning closer and closer to God. Like my spinning quarter, losing boundaries. One. One with everything.

No matter how I try, how hard I pedal in the hot, ugly room, this is all so far beyond me, and yet I *do* see angels.

I check for Colin in the mirror. He is there.

I catch Colin watching me, but his look is glancing. I can't read the expression in the mirror, and I try to imagine what I must look like from the back, dressed in elastic black, my waist pulled into a persistent hourglass above my hard-pedaling booty. I'm not twenty, but neither have I given up. Thus, the glancing look I intercept could be Colin, my own Colin, saying hello, or it could be the kid just trying to see what I look like from the front. The only way to find out what he's thinking is to ask him after class, and I'm not going to do that—because I don't know how.

"Sixty seconds. You can do this. Give me everything you've got." Celeste tells me what I already know. Time is running out.

The buzzing flywheel right in front of my eyes is yet another steel gleam, another reflective surface in this hot box of a room that seems intent on showing me everything today. The wheel is the color of Colin's lucky rock but as flat and broad as a platter.

The song, whatever it is, stops. "That's it," Celeste says. "You're done. On time." She casts a huge, cover-girl smile around the circle of the ugly room so each of us feels as if she's smiling at us alone. "I'm so glad you were here this morning."

Yes, I think. *But who, Celeste? Who was here this morning? Do you know him?*

I go through the motions. I do a few shoulder rolls, stand up in the pedals to stretch out my calves, and then I unclip. The room stops whirring. Stands still.

We are done. On time.

I'm afraid I'll cry. I feel a well of panic. I can't let him go. What if it's really him, and I don't take my chance?

But if I speak to him, what do I say? *Hey, this is going to sound really weird, but a million years ago I had a fiancé who looked exactly like you.* Do I say also, right away, in that first flush of words, that Colin is dead? Is that too creepy? Does it even matter? Would it seem like I was trying to pick him up? Me, a black-clad cougar in a cycling class? Maybe I can just stand near him, stretching, waiting casually for the disinfectant bottle to spray down the bike, and say his name quietly, under my breath, so if I am right, if it is true, he will hear me: "Colin?"

And if it isn't Colin, if he hasn't come here to tell me something, he will simply walk away, thinking me only mildly batty or even hearing my whispered word as the rush of the swamp fan. If it *is* Colin, well, then I'll know that, too. If he hears his name, so gently spoken, and turns, finally looking me right in the eyes, a replay of that moment at the top of the spiral staircase twenty-five years ago, and answers, "Jill?"

Well then.

Well. We will have broken through the barrier between this world and the next, right?

And then what? It is too late for me to go back.

All around me, my cycling buddies balance themselves on handlebars, pulling back their ankles to stretch their quadriceps. Christina folds the fluffy beach towel she carries from home. Butch plunks down on the floor and yanks back the Velcro on both cycling shoes in one swift movement, the ripping sound loud, a tiny rupturing of the space-time continuum. The dual-sweatband lady and the tambourine lady make plans to go for coffee.

I accept the damp rag and the bottle from Dale, smile, and spray down my bike, watching Colin out of the corner of my eye. He is stuffing his shoes into a black bag. The roaring in my ears has quieted, and now Eric Clapton's voice comes through the speakers. *Would you know my na-ame if I saw you in heaven?*

Oh, for real? For real.

This is the last thing I hear as I watch Colin stride through the door. He is gone. I said nothing. I want to cry. But I don't. I wipe down the seat. I pull the rag across the handlebars.

Think of all the stories we hold that we never speak, certainly not in a room full of companionable strangers, but also just because we have learned so well how to hold them. Because that's the way we do it. We contain our pain. Loss is something to be gotten through, and grief is on a schedule.

But what if we talked to each other? *Really* talked to each other? What if the heat and the music and the pounding of the blood in our hearts brought the stories spinning out of us? Maybe Dale, who was in the air force, saw his best buddy's plane take a hit and spiral out of the sky before his eyes. Maybe Butch—a charming middle-aged bachelor in a do-rag—could tell us stories about growing up Black in Middletown, USA, that would change us forever. And maybe Christina, who goes regularly to visit her grandson in Chicago, lost a child to illness, a long, long time ago. When we come together in a room like this, the hot air swims with our unspoken stories.

What if we could hear them all at once?

Colin came to see me, and I let him leave.

Instead of crying, I reach toward Mike with the spray bottle, the now soaking rag, and I say, "See you later, Mike. Have a great day."

"You too, Jill. Be careful out there."

By noon, the snow has stopped and the sun has emerged. The world transforms from menacing winter to bright spring day. Mark and I decide we will go. We pack our suitcase and the kids in the car and head south to the cabin.

I fold my toes in their warm socks under me and hold a paper cup of cappuccino to my lips. "The weirdest thing happened this morning in spinning class," I say to Mark. "This guy who looked *exactly* like Colin came into the class. I mean *exactly*."

"Like Colin then or Colin now?" Mark asks.

"Colin then," I say. "Twenty-two-year-old Colin."

"What did you do?"

"Nothing. I mean, I didn't know what to do. I wondered, though, if he'd come to give me a message or something. Like maybe we shouldn't make the trip today in the storm."

Mark's hands tighten on the steering wheel. "Why didn't you tell me?"

"I just told you."

"But we're already in the car. We're already *driving*. We're not there yet."

This is true. We are just halfway to Brown County, but the snow has stopped, the clouds have cleared, and the sun arcs across a shining blue sky with the smooth turning of the planet Earth.

Spinning.

Everything spinning. Everything.

Acknowledgments

In dramatic and humiliating fashion, I lost the fifth-grade spelling bee on "rhythm"—a word I still cannot spell with confidence. So few vowels! How to align all those consonants with just that single "y" standing in as an interim vowel? It's too much pressure. Another irksome word is the one under which this paragraph appears. I always want to put an "e" at the center, a little "gem," but I don't live in England—and really, is "acknowledgments" even the right word? Mightn't this page or two near the end of the book where you've flipped to find your name (hello, you!), or perhaps to glean a little bonus information about the company I keep, be more appropriately called "A Bucket of Gratitude" or "A Tremendous Outpouring of Exuberant Thanks"—or even, simply, "Big Love"?

That's it. This is a love story at the end of a love story. I don't want anyone to feel left out. So let's just start there: you are not forgotten. During the fifteen years it has taken to write these essays, I have lived such a good life. So many of you wrote with me or inspired me or gave me something good to eat or read or drink. You believed in me or challenged me or grieved with me. Because of you, I thrived, and where there was once nothing, now there is this book. In so many ways, y'all loved me into art, and I am so grateful.

Thank you to all the talented people at the University of Nebraska Press, but most especially Courtney Ochsner, who championed these essays from the beginning and was unfailingly smart, kind, and patient. I looked forward to every interaction. Thank you to Sara Springsteen for her gentleness and precision, and to Rosemary Sekora for her good work getting this book into many hands. To have my first collection come out in the American Lives Series, where I learned to write essays, is such a joy. Thank you to the agents who have helped me navigate the tricky business of writing—Marianne Merola and Howard Yoon. Huge thanks to Ball State University and the National Endowment for the Arts for granting me the precious gift of time.

To my many writing teachers, in and out of the classroom, but extra love to Sandy Huss, John Keeble, and Michael Martone. Your lessons found purchase in my brain. I try to pass them on.

Thank you to all my wonderful friends and colleagues, especially: Tim Berg, Cindy Collier, Pat Collier, Sarah Domet, Molly Ferguson, Ashley C. Ford, Jennifer Freyd, Rachel Hartley-Smith, Steve Harvey, Kate Hopper, Sonya Huber, Dan Lehman, Sean Lovelace, Joe Mackall, Todd McKinney, Ander Monson, Dinty W. Moore, Beth (Bich Minh) Nguyen, Bob Nowatzki, Lauren Onkey, Alysia Sawchyn, Ira Sukrungruang, Susan Taylor, and Kathy Winograd.

To the friends who sustain me. Sherrie, thank you for going back to Plum Island with me. Diane, you are the best bestie a girl could ever hope to find waiting for her in an Honors College library. Debbie and Jackie, you are my coven. I couldn't do this world without you and your wild magic.

To Carol, Sophia, and Juliet, the Neely family I'm so lucky to call my own. Sky-sent gratitude to Wright Neely (1939–2017), who copyedited my first memoir when I'd been dating his son for only a couple of years—that was brave of both of us. Bottomless thanks to my sisters, India and Sierra; my brothers, Ian and Max; their quirky, artsy, inspiring families; and the pappy we miss with all our hearts—Pete Christman (1942–2018)—who would have read this book so carefully. Who modeled for us that we show up for art. Every day.

For my mom, who gave me the summer days and the mountain loft where much of this book was drafted—and, you know, life. I love you.

Sweet Lola (2010–21), you were the perfect dog and writing companion. Maggie May, you've got some mighty big paws to fill.

For Ella and Henry. You are the reason for all of this, for everything. You are my heart.

And for Mark, my love, my life, my collaborator in so many things it's getting silly. Look at everything we've made together— this book, sure, but also: these children, our home, this lucky life. We are for each other.

Source Acknowledgments

I am deeply, enduringly grateful to the wise, generous editors of all the publications listed here who first believed in my essays and guided their development: Zoë Bossiere, Hattie Fletcher, Roxane Gay, Lee Gutkind, Martha Holloway, Laura Julier, Dan Lehman, Sam Ligon, Joe Mackall, Dinty W. Moore, Patricia Colleen Murphy, Marc Nieson, Jim Ross, and Marcelle Soviero. Your attention was invaluable. Thank you for never letting me flinch on my way to the truest story I could tell—and for asking the right questions at the right time, like this one from Joe: "Linger in the uncertainty here?"

"The Sloth" was originally published in *Brevity* 26 (Winter 2008) and was subsequently published in *The Best of* BREVITY: *Twenty Groundbreaking Years of Flash Nonfiction*, ed. Zoë Bossiere and Dinty W. Moore (Boston: Rose Metal Press, 2020).

"Going Back to Plum Island" was originally published in *River Teeth: A Journal of Nonfiction Narrative* 17, no. 1 (November 2015) and was subsequently published in *River Teeth: Twenty Years of Creative Nonfiction*, ed. Dan Lehman and Joe Mackall (Albuquerque: University of New Mexico Press, 2020).

"The River Cave" was originally published in *River Teeth: A Journal of Nonfiction Narrative* 11, no. 1 (Fall 2009).

"Bird Girls" was originally published in *Willow Springs* 68 (Fall 2011).

"Life's Not a Paragraph" was originally published as "Life's Not a Paragraph: A Literary Love Story" in *River Teeth: A Journal of Nonfiction Narrative* 19, no. 2 (June 2018).

"Family Portrait" was originally published in *Superstition Review* 8 (Fall 2011) and was revised and reprinted as "That's What You Remember: An Essay in Third Person" in *In Season: Stories of Discovery, Loss, Home, and Places In Between*, ed. Jim Ross (Gainesville: University Press of Florida, 2018).

"The Eleven-Minute Crib Nap" was originally published in *Oh Baby! True Stories About Tiny Humans*, ed. Lee Gutkind (Pittsburgh PA: In Fact Books, 2015).

"The Googly Eye" was originally published in *Brain, Child: The Magazine for Thinking Mothers* 19, no. 3 (Summer 2014).

"A Stone Pear" was originally published in *The Fourth River* 3 (Autumn 2006).

"Leading the Children Out of Town" was originally published in *Brain, Child: The Magazine for Thinking Mothers*, October 2015.

"Slaughterhouse Island" was originally published in *Not That Bad: Dispatches from Rape Culture*, ed. Roxane Gay (New York: HarperPerennial, 2018).

"The Avocado" was originally published in *Fourth Genre: Explorations in Nonfiction* 16, no. 1 (Spring 2014).

"The Baby and the Alligator" was originally published in *TriQuarterly* 151 (January 2017), a publication of Northwestern University.

"Naked Underneath Our Clothes" was originally published as "We're Naked Underneath Our Clothes" in *Creative Nonfiction* 67 (June 2018).

"Spinning" was originally published in *True Story* (Creative Nonfiction Foundation), September 2017.

The Fortune Teller's Kiss
by Brenda Serotte

Gang of One: Memoirs
of a Red Guard
by Fan Shen

Just Breathe Normally
by Peggy Shumaker

How to Survive Death and
Other Inconveniences
by Sue William Silverman

The Pat Boone Fan Club: My Life
as a White Anglo-Saxon Jew
by Sue William Silverman

Scraping By in the Big Eighties
by Natalia Rachel Singer

Sky Songs: Meditations on
Loving a Broken World
by Jennifer Sinor

In the Shadow of Memory
by Floyd Skloot

Secret Frequencies: A
New York Education
by John Skoyles

The Days Are Gods
by Liz Stephens

Phantom Limb
by Janet Sternburg

This Jade World
by Ira Sukrungruang

When We Were Ghouls: A
Memoir of Ghost Stories
by Amy E. Wallen

Knocked Down: A High-
Risk Memoir
by Aileen Weintraub

Yellowstone Autumn: A Season of
Discovery in a Wondrous Land
by W. D. Wetherell

This Fish Is Fowl: Essays of Being
by Xu Xi

To order or obtain more information on these or other University
of Nebraska Press titles, visit nebraskapress.unl.edu.

9 781496 232359